Training

Blandford Management Series
General editor: Geoffrey J. Athill, MBE, FMS, MIAM, AMBIM

TRAINING
Michael Jinks

FINANCE
Dennis Parkinson

Blandford Management Series

Training
Michael Jinks

BLANDFORD PRESS
Poole   Dorset

First published in the U.K. 1979

*Copyright © 1979 Blandford Press Ltd,
Link House, West Street,
Poole, Dorset BH15 1LL*

*ISBN 0 7137 0958 8 (Case)
     0 7137 1036 5 (Limp)*

*All rights reserved. No part of this book may
be reproduced or transmitted in any form or by
any means, electronic or mechanical, including
photocopying, recording or by any information
storage and retrieval system, without permission
in writing from the publisher.*

Jinks, Michael L.
   Training – (Blandford management studies series).
   1. Employees, Training of
   I. Title
   658.31'24   HF5549.5.T7

*Set in 11/12 pt V.I.P. Baskerville and printed and bound
by Fakenham Press Limited, Fakenham, Norfolk*

Contents

1	**Why Train?**	1
2	**Who Needs Training?**	6
3	**How do Trainees Learn?**	12
4	**Why do Trainees Learn?**	23
5	**First Steps** – A Systematic Approach to Planning	30
6	**Analysing Jobs**	36
7	**Analysing Tasks**	44
8	**Preparing to Instruct** – Written Work	52
9	**Preparing to Instruct** – Displays and Visual Aids	62
10	**Choosing the Right Method** – Imparting Knowledge and Changing Attitudes	74
11	**Choosing the Right Method** – Imparting Skills	83
12	**Do-It-Yourself Learning** – Programmed and Experiential Instruction	88
13	**Instructional Technique**	96
14	**Monitoring Trainees' Performance and Analysing Faults**	110
15	**The Training of Supervisors and Managers**	121
16	**Does Your Training Work?** – Reviewing Effectiveness	130
17	**Administering Training**	141

Contents

18	**Training Agencies, Associations and Information**	155
19	**Recapitulation**	162
	Index	173

Chapter One
Why Train?

The essential elements in any commercial enterprise are materials, equipment and manpower. Training, allied to the other human resource specialisms within management, ensures a pool of manpower of the required levels of expertise at the right time.

Or rather it should do so. Firstly, consider the attention and planning given by the average organization to the provision of materials, machinery and equipment. Then compare the commitment to the third, essential factor in the production cycle – manpower. In many industries, the manufacturing or production people expect the right sort of staff to fall from the sky in a labour crisis, and when they do not, the training department is blamed.

Why is this so? One of the most important factors is the traditional view of training and trainers. They are seen as an expense, a service, a second-rate cousin to production or a necessary evil, especially in those industries which commonly employ semi- or unskilled labour. Training has tended to follow behind other management activities, especially in the planning phase. It is often carried out as a reaction to immediate needs, a patching up operation in many cases, instead of an ordered activity.

One remedy for these traditional attitudes is to convince top management that training is properly a principal management function, which it obviously is if we accept the fact that people are a company's greatest asset. Another remedy is for trainers to display an increasing professionalism and so demand a chance for their voice to be heard at top level, along with other human resource managers, and ensure that their status is not merely as a 'side-kick' to the personnel people. The selection of trainers is still of some concern; the training department is still seen as a pasture to corral work horses who for some reason are not going to make it (or who have made it for too long) in some traditional undertakings.

The image of training in the concern is often based on conceptions of cost-effectiveness, and rightly so. The alternate view of training as a 'welfare' activity tends to wither and die in the face of troughs in the trade cycle, so training must be an activity open to the analytical eye of the accountant. Yet, in some respects, it is and always will be an act of faith to pass on one's knowledge, skills and attitudes to those who follow, and a climate in which learning is seen to be an important part of work is not easily generated by those who merely see training as a budget-balancing exercise.

What is Training?

Training is an organized procedure which brings about a semi-permanent change in behaviour, for a definite purpose. The three main areas involved are skills, knowledge and attitudes (sometimes called social skills), but always with the objective of a definite purpose in mind. It differs from education in many ways, but for all practical purposes training is aimed at specific, job-based objectives rather than the broader society-based aims of education.

Historically, trainees were expected to learn their jobs by 'exposure', i.e. by picking up what they could from experienced fellow employees. They were not termed trainees since systematic training did not occur, but enjoyed such titles as helpers, learners, improvers or mates, in industrial circles and juniors or students (among other things) in commerce.

There is no doubt that people learned their jobs in this way, but it was haphazard, learning time was lengthy, motivational needs often neglected and many incorrect procedures could be passed on. There was also a certain fear from experienced members of the work force that passing on their skills would ultimately lead to their own demise, so they tended to restrict learners' activities to menial tasks and to retain key factors about job skills until retirement.

Two world wars and intermittent periods of prosperity emphasized the need for more systematic means of training for job skills, especially in the reduction of learning time. Thus was born a more analytical approach to training and it is useful at this point to look at the selling points of a systematic training scheme.

Benefits of Systematic Training

Meeting manpower needs
When skills are required of a specific order, it is often impracticable for a concern to recruit skilled personnel on the outside labour market, so 'do-it-yourself' is the only way.

Reduced learning time
When skills and knowledge are systematically taught, the trainees are brought to efficient performance more quickly than if they had to proceed by trial and error ('exposure').

Improved performance
The elimination of incorrect working procedures and poor work habits by skilled trainers ensures only the best methods are taught. It can also apply to those already in post if acceptance is gained.

Reduced wastage
Material and equipment costs can be often dramatically cut by the installation of an efficient training scheme.

Less absenteeism
A major cause of staying at home from work, particularly with new staff, comes from not having a clear knowledge of one's duties and how to perform them.

Fewer accidents
Accidents among untrained persons are three times those among trained staff. The Health and Safety at Work Act includes specific responsibilities for trainers.

Why Train?

Reduced labour turnover
Although this is one of the more difficult 'spin-offs' of systematic training to prove, surveys have shown the labour turnover of trained staff as being only half that of untrained staff. However many other personnel department policies affect these figures, e.g. wage rates, conditions of service etc., and training officers find this a difficult area in which to claim rewards.

Benefits to employees
Any increase in job skills adds to the market value of the trainee, and can lead to advancement both within and outside the company. (One of the oft-quoted reasons for not training is the poaching of trained staff by other firms, but this is largely spurious since firms that train will usually pay well as a cogent personnel policy.)

There is also the opportunity for the employee of increased earnings in some instances, plus the inevitable job satisfaction that results from tasks performed correctly first time. Lastly there is the knowledge that the employer is sufficiently interested in their staff to take the trouble to operate systematic training.

Thus we can see several cost benefits in systematic training, but these have been known for years. In spite of the advent of the Industrial Training Act and its products, the Industrial Training Boards (ITBs), there are still firms that neglect their training function. When asked why, they present some familiar attitudes. The leviable company that spurns its ITB's approaches with the remark that they are too busy producing to waste time on training people. 'We would rather view the levy as another form of tax than muck about like that' was uttered in my presence by a rather paternalistic, but hidebound employer. There is a view also prevalent (in times of unemployment) that training people is a waste of money – just offer 'them' more cash and 'they' can be found, and other remarks along the lines that small concerns cannot afford to train.

However, wise employers see training as a long-term investment. Moreover the relationship between investment in people in terms of training and increased profit margins is clearly demonstrable, but it means waiting and faith. Above all it needs skilled practitioners with up-to-date training techniques to produce the results that are anticipated and it is hoped that the following chapters will form guidelines on sound training programmes for such people.

Chapter Two

Who Needs Training?

Formulating Policy

If training is, as we discussed in the last chapter, to be relevant and cost-effective, it must meet the needs of the organization in terms of its target population. It is pointless training for the sake of it or leaving it to chance, and the planning of who is going to receive training is essential. It is also important to plan how much they will receive and when. Considerations of who will carry out the training and the facilities that the company has at its disposal, are important factors in the planning phase.

However, the obvious first step must be to formulate a training policy, and, to bear the right fruit, this should come from the highest level of decision making in the organization. The company's approach to training, its commitment in terms of staff and facilities and the allocation of duties to line and staff appointments in terms of their training role are all decisions which need to come from the top. Consultation with Industrial Training Board advisers, where they exist, is a good thing at the beginning, so that a claim for a grant does not present problems. The company must also set the 'climate' for training in their organization by publicizing their decisions and their intentions for staff training. (Note the 'spin-off' effect upon recruitment in companies where a good training scheme exists, usually by word of mouth, e.g. Marks & Spencer.)

The next step, after this statement of intent from the top, is a careful examination of where the actual training needs really exist within the concern. This assessment of training needs is essential if the firm wishes to build up an accurate picture of the gaps in the knowledge and skills of the work force, and should be carried out with care, with professional help if need be from specialist trainers or ITB staff. Since this is not a 'one-off' exercise, the knowledge of how to go about identifying training needs will have to be vested in several key people in the training system, so a concerted approach at this stage often bears the best results.

What is a training need?
A training need is the gap between the knowledge, skills and attitudes that the job demands, and the knowledge, skills and attitudes already possessed by the trainee. It exists at all levels of the organization; it is only the emphasis on one or the other aspect which changes whether one is grooming a new chairman or instructing an operator, since knowledge, skill and attitudes are the three criteria around which all jobs are based. In the assessment of training needs, it is impossible to overstress the need for a 'gestalt' or overall view of the company's aims, objectives and manpower needs, since this exercise often determines the priorities for implementing training which can of course be critical.

Where do training needs occur?
There are three major areas in which staff display such gaps as we mentioned earlier, i.e. they are not meeting job requirements. These are (a) when their performance in their present position does not match up with the required standards – this could well be no fault of their own, e.g. new starters, (b) when the requirements of the job change due to changing circumstances and (c) when the present job ceases to exist or the job holder changes jobs, therefore creating new 'gaps' in a new job.

It is obvious from the foregoing, that no assessment of training need is going to be successful without a thorough knowledge of the job itself in all its aspects and a thorough knowledge of the personal achievements of the job holder. It is this second factor where the identification of training needs is often unsuccessful, since the investigator has not the required facts in his possession.

The collation of the necessary information about the job is fairly straightforward and can be carried out with Job Analysis,

Who Needs Training?

which we will discuss later. (It becomes more difficult where the skills involved in successfully carrying out the job are in the bracket we called attitudes or social skills. In this area charismatic influences often affect performance and are elusive to quantify to say the least. The social skills and attitudes in, say, running a public house or teaching adults are difficult to put down on paper as indeed are many 'management' functions, whereas in the areas of manipulative skills and job knowledge, precise information is available.)

However, the collation of the information about how many of the necessary qualities the jobholder (or candidate) already possesses is often the more difficult to ascertain. In my experience, face-to-face interview techniques by the assessor are most profitable, although not always practicable. Where questionnaires, forms and other non-personal techniques are used, there seems always to be a lack of important feedback on attitudes and performance standards, often psychological in nature, which cannot be determined in writing. However the sheer numbers of the target population for the survey sometimes precludes much else, but it seems obvious that a skilled interviewer will elicit more of the detail that is required for successful indentification of the 'gaps'.

What questions need the assessor ask?
Firstly, the would-be investigator needs to know the position in the company as a whole at the present moment with regard to staffing and needs to find out the answers to the following questions:

> Who do we employ?
> Where? How do they fit into the concern?
> What categories do we place them in?
> Who takes them on and how often?
> Where do they come from?
> How long do they stay?
> Why do they leave?
> (Most of the above information should be readily available from the personnel section.)
> What jobs do they do?

Who Needs Training?

Is there a job description?
What are they supposed to do – and what is actually done?
What standards are set?
Are they being met?
If not, why not?
Who trains at present, and do staff learn properly?
Are the current key problems in teaching targets:
    quantity?
    quality?
    working conditions?
How cost-effective is our present training?

Secondly, any changes in the future will usually bring about training needs, so research will have to be carried out to forecast developments that are to occur. This area of 'crystal-balling' is a function of successful management planning but always seems to be the area least well tackled in training needs analysis, especially in companies employing no training specialist, where line managers responsible for their own internal training often fail to take 'time-out' to review their future needs. (One line manager I knew with his work force of 75% over fifty-five years of age, had taken no steps to secure replacement of skilled operators and I expect the reader can think of many similar examples.)

What future needs will force the company to train, or retrain?

Expansion.	Promotions.
Reorganization.	Seasonal variations.
New methods.	Change in layout.
New equipment.	Special jobs.
New legislation.	Changes in manning
New products.	levels.
Retirements.	New managements, etc.

These are just examples of the sort of information the trainer must have at his fingertips to be able to assess accurately the 'gaps' in people's skills, knowledge and attitudes in the future. It is helpful quite often to attempt to place them in order of priority as to whether they are (a) potential needs, (b) pending needs or (c) current needs which have been overlooked.

Fault Correction

Lastly, if any justification is wanted to underline the need for an analysis of the gaps in people's skills, let us examine the costs of not training or training insufficiently in the first instance. Poor performance due to shortage of skills can result in many problems, the symptoms of which are legion but may include:

Customer complaints.	Inaccurate records.
Wastage.	Production holdups
Abuse of equipment.	('bottlenecks').
Disregard of safety rules.	Rise in reject rates.

All of these will require some remedial training input, which is wasteful, costly and difficult, since often it involves 'unlearning' poor work habits, due to inefficient instruction at the initial demonstration phase. This can be very time consuming, since most people have great difficulty in 'unlearning' habits. Note that these latter training needs cannot be forecasted, are therefore not included on any training plan and hence will cause undefinable extra workloads on trainers. This is of paramount importance where a manager is doing his own instruction, where time taken in fault correction (because that is what it is, in the main) has to be stolen from other more dynamic activities. Fault correction is a major cause of supervisory frustration, and so any reduction in this activity by more systematic instruction during initial training is bound to affect the productivity and morale of a department.

To summarize, a training need is present when there is a gap between the knowledge, skills and attitudes displayed by people in their jobs and the knowledge, skills and attitudes which are required for them to achieve the results the job needs, both now and in the future.

Training Forecasts

We have looked at where such gaps typically occur – with new staff, when existing staff need retraining because of new circumstances and when faults cause the trainer to correct

Who Needs Training?

things on the spot. The conclusion is that the majority of these training needs can be foretold and the manager who spends time analysing his training needs, or the trainer who provides such a service for him, will be amply repaid by increased performance in the future. It is obvious that such a survey as we have been discussing should result in some sort of training forecast.

The training forecast is a list of priorities, the factors involved being:

1. Key areas which closely affect the success of the company.
2. Estimates of the duration and type of training for each specified job.
3. The number of trainees required to fill those jobs.
4. Present availability of training staff.
5. The need to provide additional instructional help.
6. Suitable locations (if necessary) for siting a training area.
7. Any outside specialist help necessary.
8. A cost estimate of the proposals.
9. A cost benefit estimation of the training proposed (in terms of savings).

In this way one arrives at an estimated forecast of the training activity necessary to meet the training needs and paves the way for the next step in the process – preparing a training plan. However, before starting this systematic approach, it would be useful to remind ourselves of the process by which trainees learn (and especially the motivational factors that influence why they do so) since this formation will be invaluable during the planning process. Training has been described as planning to give people the chance to learn to achieve the results that the job demands, so it seems opportune at this point to refresh our memories on the way people learn, not just as new trainees but throughout their lives.

Chapter Three

How do Trainees Learn?

It has been said by many teachers, not least of them Einstein, that 'we cannot teach anyone anything, we can only help them to learn'. In essence, this is the core of the trainer's work – the provision of the optimum conditions for trainee's learning. In order to provide this climate in which learning can take place, the trainer must understand some very basic principles of the learning process. This is not an exhaustive treatise on learning, much of the information can be found in greater detail elsewhere in specialist books; this is merely a practical view of the ways in which a trainer can aid his trainees in their acquisition of skill and knowledge.

Incoming stimuli are transmitted to the brain by means of the senses. This incoming information is often referred to as the *receptor* process and the receptive senses can be listed as follows:

Sight
The most important sense from a learning point of view as it is estimated that sight provides between 70–85% of the important stimuli used in the learning process.

Hearing
Another important factor, often concerned with knowledge acquisition through talks, lectures, discussion and the sounds associated with skill stimuli.

Touch
Most important in skill acquisition is the sense of feel; objects, surfaces and textures being typical incoming stimuli.

Smell
This sense is often used as a monitoring device, e.g. the recognition of danger signals such as burning etc. and also in the setting of standards (e.g. in cooking).

Taste
The sampling of materials can be a powerful sensory stimulant and an important aid to learning, especially in catering and medicine.

Kinaesthesis
This sense often hard to define, but undoubtedly present, is often called the 'sense of muscular feel'. It is demonstrated during balancing, pushing, pulling and pressing. By experience we have an innate knowledge of how much muscular effort we need to exert to perform a certain action. Sometimes we are surprised, for instance when a case has been unloaded without our knowledge, or the door closer removed and we exert far too much effort. (Perhaps it is easier to demonstrate its existence by noting when it misleads us!) Obviously kinaesthesis is important in the co-ordinating mechanisms of skill acquisition, and has much to do with practice.

Another key factor in the receptor phase is perception. Perception is not the same as the use of the senses, since perceiving something implies that we attach meaning to the stimulus, and can relate it to previous incoming information. Perhaps a way to illustrate perception is to note the ability of trained people to differentiate between minute differences in sensory information and to relate it in a meaningful way. A skilled cutter in the footwear industry can look at a piece of leather, predict its wear qualities and so place his pattern accordingly. An ornithologist can distinguish certain types of bird from a flock which are apparently identical to the lay viewer. There is a discriminatory factor about perception, and it differs from individual to individual in its power. So obviously perception is important in skill acquisition particularly the ability to perceive what is important to the satisfactory completion of the task, from what are merely background factors. Good trainers help learners'

How do Trainees Learn?

perception by pointing out these key factors, coaching them into perceiving what is essential and what is not. Sometimes we have a 'natural' – someone who instinctively perceives very quickly the very fine discriminatory impulses necessary to achieve the task and who can repeat the experience at will.

The receptor stage can be summarized diagrammatically as in fig. 1.

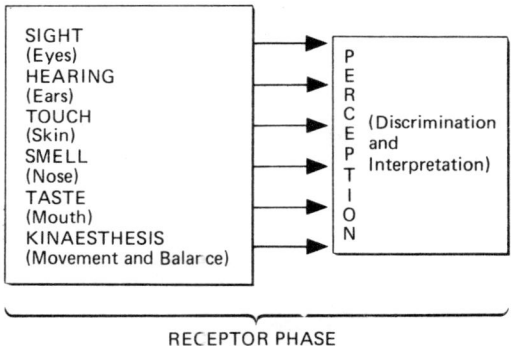

Fig. 1 The receptor process.

Before leaving perception it is useful to note that many external and internal factors can affect the levels of perception in the same individual such as:

Health.	Distractions.
Fatigue.	Motivation.
Memory.	Overfamiliarity.
Levels of lighting.	Prior expectations.

These factors may affect the subsequent interpretation of the incoming sensory stimuli at different times.

The incoming sensory information is processed by the brain and is organized into coherent action impulses, mainly through

How do Trainees Learn?

muscular movement. The middle phase, i.e. the brain operating upon the sensory stimuli, we could for want of a better word call the *cognitor* processes though this is a vast oversimplification of what, even to scientists, is a not too easily understood phenomenon. However to the practical manager this cerebral part of the learning process is very observable, if not academically describable. The learner cyclist for instance, reaching his first bend in the road, may tend to lean too far over on approach. However the brain corrects the action necessary in successful 'judgement' and the learning process takes place. This shows that not only does the brain exercise judgement, but also has a storage facility we term memory.

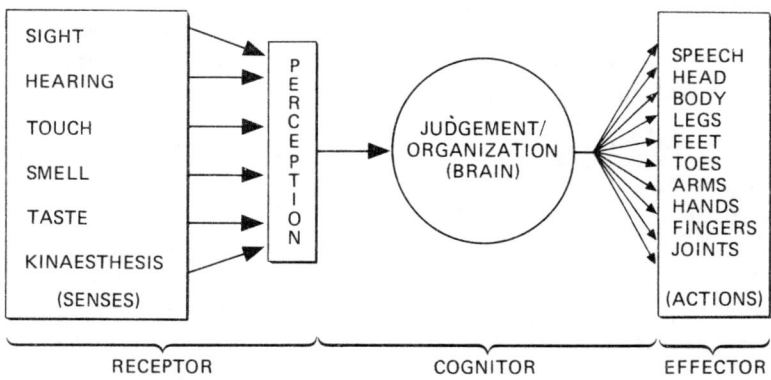

Fig. 2 *The learning system.*

The third phase of the process can be termed the *effector* or action phase, when instructions from the brain operate the motor functions of the nervous system and culminate in muscle movement. Skills are sometimes referred to as 'sensorimotor' skills and we can see why, since the sense control incoming stimuli, judgement occurs and the motor system in the body is operated. Thus they are not simply patterns of movement, but are subject to the intellect in the middle phase. The effector channels are the limbs and faculties of the body and consist of:

Speech.	Arms.
Head.	Fingers.
Body.	Toes.
Legs.	Joints.
Feet.	

A diagrammatic representation of the entire system might now look like fig. 2.

Factors Affecting the Learning Process

Knowledge of results
This is one of the major factors influencing the rate at which trainees learn. The ability of the brain to correct inaccurate motor functions is an obvious way in which this rate is influenced, but by and large, the quicker the feedback to the trainee, the more quickly will he learn. In learning theory this is often referred to as 'reinforcement'. However, over-informing the trainee, particularly at the beginning, of his failures is liable to affect his motivation (see next chapter).

Length of learning sessions
There is evidence to show that, for the same amount of practice, spaced learning gives better results than massed learning, i.e. reasonably short periods of practice are better than long ones. This is believed to be a result of the brain's need of time to organize the incoming stimuli during the interim periods and to pass information from short- to long-term memory in the storage facility. However the optimum time between practice sessions and the length of session itself will vary with the individual trainee and can only be determined by trial and error.

Part versus whole learning
Generally, the smaller the amount of new material presented to the trainee at one time the quicker and more effectively will he learn. This is because the sensory system can cope with only a certain amount of incoming stimuli at one time, otherwise the

How do Trainees Learn?

organizing mechanisms in the brain become overloaded with too many signals. Individual components of a job can be broken down into easily assimilable steps to ensure that this overloading does not occur. Again the amount of material that is digested will differ from trainee to trainee, but the good trainer will always be looking analytically at tasks to find the optimum amount of new learning to include at each stage.

Logical sequence
Information which is given or stages which are instructed in a logical sequence are much more easily recalled than random presentation. The retrieval system in the brain is helped if incoming stimuli are organized for the trainee by the instructor. The lesson here for the trainer is obvious – clear, sequential presentation of material and visual aids organized into efficient memory cues should be used. Adequate preparation is the only way to secure these benefits.

Depth of impression
Recall is closely associated with the vividness or depth of impression of past experiences. Imagery, i.e. the presentation of learning material in imaged object form can transform dull knowledge-type training sessions into memorable experiences for trainees. Charts, diagrams and statistics, for example, can be more easily learned with vivid graphic presentation. Lasting impressions can be achieved during instruction by realism, novelty, competition and curiosity thereby keeping the attention of the trainee as well as aiding his recall.

Repetition
The opportunity to rehearse and practise a skill, and its effect upon subsequent improved performance has been noted for centuries. 'Practice makes perfect' was the old adage, and it is true that frequent performance of a skill induces automatic responses from the effector mechanisms, which we term habits. However, whilst the trainer should ensure that sufficient opportunities are allowed for the trainee to repeat his skill, it is important that the correct habits are repeated, since bad habits are just as easily learned by repetition as good ones. Trainers

are in business to ensure that the automatic reactions of trainees are the correct ones, so careful monitoring of trainee's practice sessions is essential.

Association of ideas
Learning takes place more effectively if we can associate new knowledge with that already possessed. Past experience of the same or similar learning situations is a basis for the trainer to link in new information, since the trainee can relate his new knowledge (i.e. the organizing part of his brain can recall similar past stimuli, thus speeding the sorting and assimilation stage). The trainer therefore must carefully check previous knowledge, and find existing skills on which to graft the new material.

Transfer of learning
It would be sensible to suppose that trainees who have mastered one type of job would find it easy to learn a similar series of tasks. However it does not necessarily follow, the crucial factor being the amount of identical elements in the two tasks. For example a trained typist would be relatively easy to train on a teleprinter, but a typist learning to play the piano would find it almost as difficult to learn as would a beginner.

The trainer's task then is to analyse the similar element in old and new tasks and to concentrate his efforts on the new or strange factors which the trainee will not find so easy. Where the trainee finds it easier to learn the new task because of previous experience we call this positive transfer. However, previously learned material can sometimes cause inferior performance, where automatic reactions have been set up, as discussed in the earlier paragraph, and temporary losses of performance occur due to old habits, e.g. when a car driver from the Continent arrives in Britain he tends to drive on the right-hand side of the road for a while (ask Southampton policemen!). This process is called negative transfer and trainers should be aware that there are occasions in the learning process when possession of certain skills can actually constitute a handicap to the learning of a new skill.

Transfer problems also occur when trainees have to move

from a training school situation to the real live working area. There is often a steep fall in performance due to surrounding influences even though the work is as similar as it is possible to make it. This of course constitutes one of the valid arguments in having as much training as is possible in the actual working situation, i.e. on-job instruction where the real tempo and environment can be perceived by the trainee. (Note that this is probably a foul-up in the perception link in the learning process.)

Learning Curves

The usual way in which we trace the pick-up of sensorimotor skills is by plotting the process on a graph called a learning curve. This mainly shows decreasing gains in skill pick-up as time goes on. A curve like fig. 3 is typical.

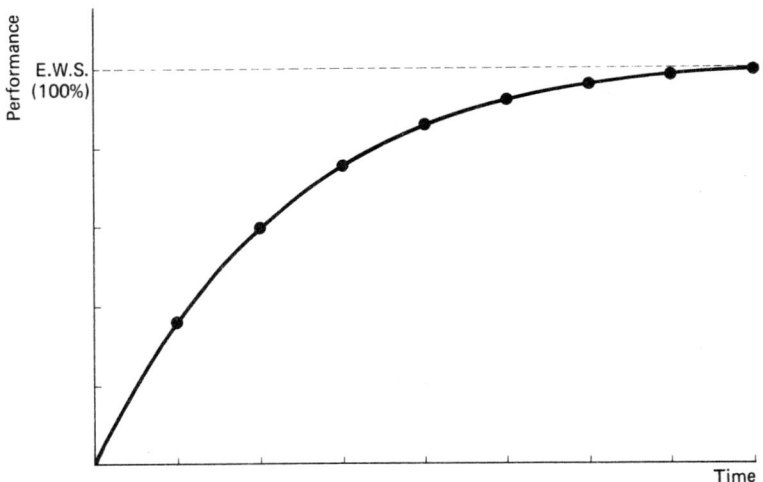

Fig. 3   The learning curve.

This tends to be a little discouraging to the learner, but explanation will clearly show that the most dramatic skill pick-ups will occur initially and relatively minor improvements

How do Trainees Learn?

will come as mastery approaches. Thus the nearer the trainee is to experienced worker standard (sometimes referred to as EWS) the greater need he will have for the coaching and encouragement of his trainer, a factor overlooked by people new to instructional techniques.

Plateaux on Learning Curves

In many skill-type training programmes instead of the curve showing the expected decreasing gains, a time comes where there appears to be no visible improvement from one attempt to another or even for several attempts and a plateau occurs in the learning as in fig. 4.

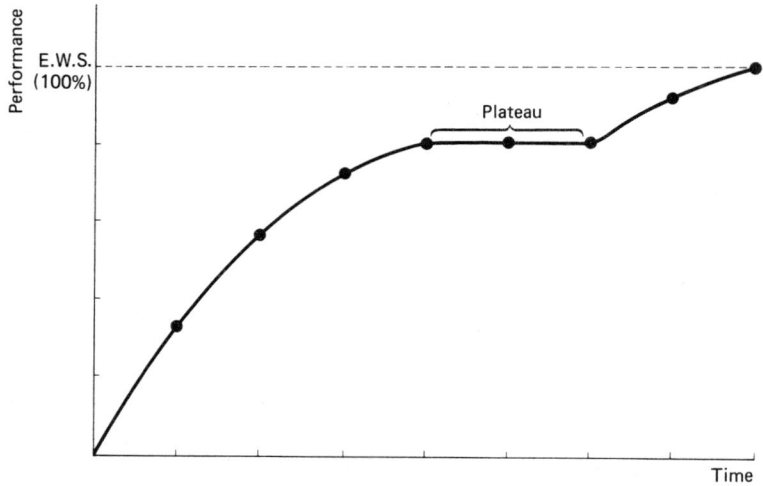

Fig. 4   The learning curve plateau.

These plateaux represent difficult times for the trainee and they usually occur because a qualitative change during practice has taken place, often due to a perception difficulty, resulting in an imperceptible change in method. The trainer will need to analyse carefully where the learning conflict is taking place to coach the trainee into further improvement, or the trainee may give up with the comment, 'I'll never get the hang of this.' Sometimes referred to in the vernacular as 'the knack', a sudden comprehension of the co-ordination of the effector processes is often the key to solving these plateaux. The trainer must be analytical and, above all, patient during such phases, being prepared for frequent re-demonstration.

Overlearning

Something which is to be retained for a long period needs to be learned beyond the point of bare recall, i.e. the skill is not learned only to bare mastery, but repeated beyond this point. When we think of some of the skills we learn in childhood (e.g. cycling, swimming), there is no wonder that we can retain them, even after years of dis-use, when we consider the amount of 'overlearning' which took place. The acquisition of automatic reactions takes place because we practise beyond the mastery phase, continuing to perform the skill far beyond the point of original learning. The trainer has another difficulty here in persuading the learner that once mastery has been achieved, he must still practise to install automatic reactions, or he may only have a short term gain in skill pick-up.

To summarize briefly, the following principles apply in learning:

a. Trainees learn through the senses so the more senses that the trainer can appeal to, the quicker and more permanent the learning (vide the old Chinese proverb 'I hear – I forget; I see – I remember; I do – I understand').
b. Telling people how to do a task is not teaching it. Trainees must be given the chance to participate using all their senses.
c. Practice and repetition are needed to reinforce learning.
d. Knowledge of results speeds learning.
e. Spaced practice is better than massed practice for the same amount of time.
f. Generally people learn more quickly when the amount of new material is broken down into logical, easy-to-follow steps.

How do Trainees Learn?

g. Build on previous knowledge, grafting on new material to a related base.
h. People learn at different speeds. Treat people as individuals especially in the learning situation.
i. Give impact to your sessions and make them memorable by adequate, vivid preparation and presentation.
j. Proceed from the simple to the difficult, known to unknown – this aids transfer of skills.
k. Learning does not stop at bare mastery – it must proceed until automatic reactions (the correct ones!) are an inbuilt habit.
l. Be patient. Only by patience will you help people through their learning 'plateaux', which is the time when they are most likely to give up. Finally, be analytical, since only through constant observation and questioning will the trainer be in the position to correct faults and coach accordingly.

Chapter Four
Why do Trainees Learn?

In the last chapter we looked at the learning process, starting off with the premise that 'we cannot teach anyone anything, we can only help them to learn'. This presupposes that the learning process cannot begin unless the motivational desire, i.e. the will to learn is present. The trainer's task is to take this will to learn, to optimize training opportunities and to help the trainee to meet his own (and corporate) goals. To do this he must have an understanding not only of how people learn, but of the psychological factors which influence learning, particularly current thinking on motivation in the instructional field.

Goal Setting

Trainees must, if they are to be receptive to instruction, see a reason in learning the skills or knowledge we are trying to instruct. The goal is a primary factor in the amount of effort people put into their learning, so the trainer must be able to understand the goals at which his trainees are aiming, and to be able to point out other goals that the trainees may have overlooked. *Intrinsic* goals are so called because they satisfy some inner desire, the need to pass one's own inspection, giving a sense of accomplishment which derives from doing something one always wanted to do. This is obviously a powerful motivational force which helps the trainer enormously – his main task being to harness and channel the strong desire for knowledge in such trainees. *Extrinsic* motivation refers to the need for external goals being set as a reward for effort, e.g. money, praise, incentive bonuses, prestige or better working conditions. The trainer's work here is centred on arousing interest in the extrinsic goals, pointing out benefits of their attainment and sustaining effort during training by reminding and giving feedback, encouragement and reward. Both types of motivation are important to the learning process, but it will be obvious that the trainee with extrinsic goals which are well understood has a head start and will weather the difficult times during learning more successfully. However we all know that by far the most of our training work will be concerned with people requiring intrinsic rewards, particularly at the operator level, so it is important that the trainer spends adequate time on motivating learners, especially those learning jobs of an unskilled or semi-skilled nature. This can be done by ensuring that the learner knows why the task is necessary, by explaining its relevance and importance in the context of the whole job and by pointing out the rewards for successful performance.

What Needs are Satisfied at Work?

The trainer must have a basic knowledge of the needs that are satisfied during working hours so that he can pitch his instruction at appropriate goals. A working knowledge of motivational theory is also useful in the important business of gaining rapport with the trainee, as we shall see later. It is important to view trainees as individuals, whose needs will vary with age, circumstances, background and time; however a broad grouping of needs is a useful start. The basic needs of people (food, warmth, shelter etc.) can be termed existence needs and many of these can only be satisfied by work. Many jobs merely provide the trainee with a wage packet, with which he purchases his existence needs. However that is not to denigrate the worker or the job, since society depends upon jobs and job holders working at routine, undemanding tasks, and of course other needs are satisfied outside working hours.

The second grouping of needs satisfied by work can be termed social needs; the desire to conform, be part of a team, relate to others and meet group objectives. They are all pointers that man is a social animal and has 'relatedness' needs to and for others. Some of these needs are satisfied at work, mainly in group tasks, and one of the trainer's duties is that of team building.

Why do Trainees Learn?

Lastly the needs of many people at work can be seen in the context of personal fulfilment. The taxing of one's abilities, the pride in achievement and the growth that comes from meeting challenges and achieving objectives gives meaning to many jobs at all levels of society. It is not necessary to see this fulfilment in terms of high skill content since a hospital cleaner may get as great a sense of achievement from a gleaming corridor as a teacher with a brilliant pupil. It is the analysis of a trainee's needs and the joint progress through learning towards his personal targets, that form realistic, adult attitudes to fulfilment goals from the trainer's point of view.

Incentives to Greater Effort

How can the trainer maximize the need to learn? What incentives can he offer as a reward for adequate effort? We are back to extrinsic rewards for some of the more obvious incentives such as money, bonuses, better working conditions and so on but there are other incentives for successful performance that the trainer can offer, at a more personal level.

Encouragement and feedback are great incentives, if given promptly. Praise is important to the trainee in terms of ego needs and should be given freely to trainees who produce good performances. The whole process of learning can be geared to setting challenges, friendly competition and adequate rewards in the right 'climate', i.e. where the trainer has built a rapport based on mutual respect.

Pride in results, the sense of craftsmanship, is another area where the trainer sets standards of quality and performance. The need to meet the trainer's standard, i.e. the level of expectation, can be a powerful motivator in some cases, particularly where a group are working in friendly competition. One of the major incentives is of course advancement. This may be a long-term incentive in some cases but it is particularly strong in the young. The trainer's role here is often that of pointing out career opportunities in a realistic manner, ensuring that such advancement goals are within the grasp of the trainee's abilities.

Traditionally, there has always been the negative incentive

of punishment for failure. However quite often the effect is that poor responses are suppressed and not unlearned in such situations. If punishment is adjudged appropriate, immediate reinforcement of the correct response is much more effective. Constant experience of success in whatever the size of the task, is much the best incentive for most people, so the trainer must break down his instruction to provide opportunities for trainees to experience success within their own learning capacities.

The Trainer/Trainee Relationship

There is no doubt that people learn best from someone they like, and will suppress unpleasant learning experiences, probably forgetting the material being taught at the same time. Learning is fun when presented in a stimulating, enthusiastic way by a trainer who genuinely cares about the relationship between him and his trainees. There is however a two-way responsibility – no trainer can maintain this climate on his own, since he depends upon his trainee's attainments to fulfil his needs.

This understanding of mutual needs is important since the role of trainer and trainee revolves around it. The trainee needs the nurturing presence of a respected figure who provides him with a structure for his learning, monitors his performance and evaluates fairly. The trainer needs, for satisfaction in his work, the attainment of successful performance in a cheerful and willing manner by his trainees.

The trainer acts in many ways as a model, especially to young trainees. They see in him the embodiment of professional attitudes towards their work, and, consciously or unconsciously, shape their behaviour towards his. Many trainees will remember their trainer long after they have forgotten the tasks that he taught; an illustration of the special relationship with young people that the trainer enjoys. With this privilege goes ensuing responsibilities, with regard to personal habits, approach to the job, and personal mannerisms. The experienced observer can tell the origin of trainees, and the trainer under whom they learned, by these characteristics, since trainees often exhibit slavishly the mannerisms of their tutor.

Objectivity, fairness and acceptance of the rules are important factors in the psychological make-up of the successful trainer, and he should not be too much of a tyrant, for his is a powerful position. Conversely he must not be too lax in his attitude or he will fail to give the learner a sense of challenge. A good trainer finds the middle course, and will be rewarded by moments of genuine self-fulfilment for his efforts.

Anxiety in the Learning Process

No-one learns when they are fearful since this freezes performance and reduces the level of perception by the process of sensory inhibition. The very situation of learning something new arouses apprehension in many, since it is associated with past failures, fears of the schoolroom and doubts about future capabilities. The learner is vulnerable, especially those who are re-training, since we are often rated in the world according to our skills or qualifications and it is obviously 'not O.K.' if we possess none of these attributes, or inappropriate ones.

How can the trainer diminish anxiety? The first step is his manner -- a friendly, approachable style with a straightforward integrity is ideal. The use of appropriate humour is an important factor, since laughter is akin to tears as a release of pent-up anxiety. An intelligent interest in the trainee as a person, with a caring approach to his progress is also important, as is the avoidance of sarcasm in critical appraisal of their efforts. This supportive attitude helps in clarity of demonstration and provides a climate for constructive tolerance of mistakes.

Research has shown that trainees with high anxiety fare worse in the learning process than those with low anxiety. Moreover, external pressure for results tends to spur low anxiety students but not those with high anxiety. The high drive levels associated with nervousness produces responses that actually interfere with the learning process, and people who are naturally apprehensive tend to react to new situations with a fear of failure that is detrimental to performance. A trainer can help such people by designing training programmes with carefully thought out steps to success, by reducing outside environmental interference during learning, by adequate feedback and encouragement immediately after practice, by not laughing at unsuccessful attempts (or allowing other trainees to do so) and by the gradual development of confidence with systematic gradation of work from simple to difficult.

Capacity for Learning, and Age

All three parts of the learning mechanism are affected by advancing years; the senses become dulled, cerebral decay is a function of brain cells dying off and not being replaced and the effector processes are reduced as a result of increased inactivity. However, much can be done to reduce this rate of bodily decline if constant use is made of the learning facilities, and those older people who have consistently used and exercised their brain and body can expect to learn effectively until an advanced age.

An important factor in learning in older workers is the relatedness of new material to knowledge already possessed; generally the closer new skills are similar to those abilities acquired in the past (provided motivation is there) then the easier will be the assimilation of new material. Another important aspect is the relationship between age and the increased fear of the learning situation (see 'high anxiety' trainees in the foregoing paragraph). Mature trainees will suffer from an understandable reluctance to enter the challenging atmosphere of learning something new, especially if it is many years since the last formal acquisition of new skills. It is obvious from the foregoing that the trainer will have to be especially aware when dealing with older workers if he is to help them to undergo the change that is part of the training process.

In summary, trainers should:

a. Treat all learners as individuals and get to know them.
b. Use a friendly manner, approachable and straightforward, during training.
c. Try to put people at ease – no-one learns when they are nervous.

Why do Trainees Learn?

d. Remember you are a model as well as a teacher; trainees will imitate your behaviour as well as your skills.
e. Find out the goals of each learner; use them in the development of the training programme. Remember intrinsic goals are usually better than extrinsic ones.
f. Give feedback and reward effort quickly; criticize constructively, reinforcing positive responses afterwards.
g. Be especially aware of trainees with motivational problems, especially the anxious and the older student.
h. Be yourself; learning should be fun, so it is O.K. to laugh! (Besides, it reduces emotional tension.)

Chapter Five

First Steps – *A Systematic Approach to Planning*

Preparing a Training Plan

The first task in a systematic approach to training is to examine the Training Forecast that the analysis of our training needs has produced. Before our digression into the learning process in the previous two chapters, the reader will remember that we had arrived at the position where we can now list the priorities in our training.

A Training Plan does just this, representing the commitments that the company considers will be its training objectives for a stated period of time. There is no set format for such a plan since individual concerns will have different requirements. Involvement with Industrial Training Boards, where they affect a company, will determine an acceptable format in some cases, but obviously training plans will vary from elaborate productions to single sheets of foolscap, depending on the scale of training activity.

However, all training plans will need to include the following information:

> How long a period does the plan cover? (This in practice is often tied in with the company's financial strategy.)
>
> How much money has been budgeted for training activity during this time?
>
> What key result areas will be the major targets, i.e. who is going to receive training and development during the planned period and how many? (For example, which managers will need their job skills extending to achieve policy targets; how many supervisors will need instructional technique courses; which operators will need on-job training in new techniques?)

First Steps – A Systematic Approach to Planning

What type of training will meet these needs? (In broad categories such as induction, basic training, systematic analytical training, instructional technique training, supervisory skills, communications, human relations, management development etc.)

What method of training, with these broad categories, will be most suitable? (There are at least fifty different training methods to choose from in achieving objectives.)

How long will the training programme for each category last? (e.g. two half-hour sessions or five days spread over three weeks can be the time allocated to induction in differing companies.)

Where will training take place? (External courses, on-job training, mixture of both?)

Duration of training programme and target dates for completion.

Delegation of responsibility for actual carrying out the training. (Management level, supervision, on-job trainers? Don't forget to tell them!)

Follow up procedures to aid in evaluating how successful the training has been.

The training plan is only the beginning of the process, but it is a vital part in gaining acceptance and commitment at all levels of the organization and needless to say should receive maximum publication.

Training Programmes

The actual 'nuts and bolts' of the planning process end in the recording on paper of the final details of the policy in the form of a training programme. This is the 'order of battle', the authorization document and terms of reference for the trainers. Training programmes are drawn up for each category of staff as defined in the training plan, or may even be drawn up for individuals, where personal development has been decreed. Obviously the process of drawing up such programmes will involve people at the 'sharp end' ideally, that is the trainers who will actually be responsible for the day-to-day running of the programme.

All training programmes have certain core features which can be listed below, but will of course differ in emphasis depending on the position of the trainee in the hierarchy, the number of trainees and so on, but common factors are:

> Overall aim and objective of the programme, i.e. what knowledge, skills and attitudes will be instilled at the end of the training period.
>
> Subject matter to be covered (the syllabus or curriculum in some cases), in sessional form and in logical sequence.
>
> The method of training that is to be employed to cover the subject matter in sufficient detail for trainers to use, e.g. lecture, discussion, on-job demonstration, practice etc.
>
> Where and when the training will take place, in terms of duration if not actual dates.
>
> Who will do the training, i.e. the people to whom training function has been delegated.
>
> Follow-up to the session to check performance, review progress or for recording purposes.

The presentation of this information is usually a policy feature of the training organization concerned and can be of columnar format or report based, with headings and subheadings. Another factor governing the way in which the programme is presented, is the preference of the Industrial Training Board concerned (if any), since the way it is presented is often important in claiming a grant. A typical columnar approach can be seen in fig. 5, but it must be stressed that not all training programmes lend themselves to this format, particularly some management development programmes.

Factors in Programme Design

Firstly, it must be pointed out that much of the information needed to plan an effective training programme will come from job analysis, which is covered in a later chapter. Indeed it can be argued that training programmes are the end product of

TRAINING PROGRAMME

Title:— Machine Operator (Hawkins Rotary)

Objective:— To train operative (to Experienced Worker Standard in performance and quality) on the Hawkins Rotary Machine within six weeks.

SUBJECT	METHOD	LOCATION & TIME	TRAINER	FOLLOW UP
Induction	Talk and Guided Tour	Personnel Office Factory & Depts Day 1 8.30-10 am	Chief Instructor	Give out Induction booklets
Introduction to machine	Demonstration and Visual Aids	Training School Day 1 10am-12pm	Instructor No.1	Question and answer with trainees
Machine operation (1, Control)	Demonstration and practise by trainees	Training School Day 1 1 - 2 pm	Instructor No.1	Assess performance show charting method
Knowledge of company products	Lecture with samples	Sample Room Day 1 2 - 3 pm	Chief Designer	Recognition test at later date
Machine operation	Further practise	Training School Day 1 3.15-4.15pm	Instructor No.1	Chart performance

Fig. 5 Presentation of a training programme.

thinking about what the job is, what the worker does, and the best way to teach it, since the 'gaps' involved in meeting training needs involve a detailed knowledge of job methods. However, since training programmes are properly a part of the planning process, we will assume that the feedback in the training cycle (planning – implementing – reviewing) is providing the planner with the information that he needs. The reader new to training will find more detailed information on job analysis and teaching methods later in this book, enabling him to form judgements for himself on precisely where training programme design features in his own training cycle.

At whatever stage in the process the programme is drawn up, several important factors have to be borne in mind. It is essential to think back to the learning process, incorporating into the training programme the principles that we discussed in that chapter.

> The training programme must have a logical progression, enabling the trainee to recognize sequence.
>
> The programme must maintain interest for the trainee, by providing variety, mixing practical with theory sessions and allowing adequate time for discussion periods, grafting new knowledge on to old by mixing new exercises with revision of old ones, and varying instructional methods wherever possible. A new face from the training staff also helps, as does a high rate of participation by trainees.
>
> Learning is tiring, especially to school leavers, so limit input sessions to 45 minutes wherever possible, as attention tends to wander after this length of time. In skill-type instruction stamina building can be introduced by gradually lengthening the practice sessions as time goes on, but have a range of exercises so that the trainee can be moved around.
>
> Maintain flexibility in the programme by relating the rate of instructional material to the trainee's own learning capacity. All programmes should have inbuilt feedback systems to the trainer in the form of performance testing at regular intervals, so that he can adjust the flow of new material to suit individual trainees.

First Steps – A Systematic Approach to Planning

Learning by doing is best, so wherever possible make the programme active and job-related, keeping trainees occupied by learning at least one new thing every day. Use those teaching methods which allow the trainee to experience for himself the real atmosphere in which the job is carried out.

Finally, it is important that the trainee is able to see his own training programme, since it indicates to him the extent of his new learning experiences. Whilst some trainers would say that this can be 'off-putting' to some anxious trainees, in general this is far outweighed by the advantages of the trainee being able to participate in his own development.

Chapter Six

Analysing Jobs

In training needs analysis, we identified a training need as the gap between the knowledge, skills and attitudes that the job demands and those already possessed by the trainee. It is obvious therefore that the trainer must know the job in all its aspects before he can train people to do it. One of the most important ways he can get to know about the job is by job analysis.

Job Analysis

This is a process, not a document, although quite a few documents will be produced from it. It is an analytical examination of a particular occupation, since the word 'job' is taken to mean occupation as opposed to a duty or task. A 'duty' is a major area of responsibility within a job and a 'task' is a specific element by which some result is achieved. An example might be; job – bus conductor, duty – the collection of fares, task – punching tickets; or job – personnel manager, duty – selection of new staff, task – filling in interview report form.

Job analysis can be used for several purposes upon completion. In addition to its training function it can be used for method study, merit rating, job evaluation and other purposes with very little modification. Some of these other uses are rather emotive in labour relations, so it is important to stress that it is being done for training purposes (and needless to say it should be ensured that it is all that it is used for!). In essence it is finding out everything about the job that the trainer will need to know, such as:

> Purpose – why is the job done? Why does it exist at all?

Analysing Jobs

Setting – what environmental factors are there? What is the physical and social background to the job?

Facilities – what is available to the job holder in terms of back-up service, supply of materials, equipment and resources?

Execution – what duties and responsibilities are involved in successful performance of the job? What major tasks need to be carried out? (Beware not to take too fine a look at tasks at this stage or it becomes a task analysis.)

Liaison – what contacts with others does the job holder have? What social skills are involved in negotiation or liaison with other departments?

Position – what is the status of the job in the hierarchy? To and for whom is the job holder responsible?

How do we go about collecting this information? The first step is obviously to enlist the support of all concerned. If the training plan has shown that areas of company activity need a closer look, then presumably top management will be in agreement with the analytical process, but it is wise not to undertake a study without clearing it with senior managers, if only out of courtesy. Middle management and supervisors will need a more careful explanation of aims objectives and methods before a start can be made, and trade union representatives will need special briefing. (In these days of 'differentials' in job grading being a highly political issue, great care must be taken in proving the training intent.) If an operator is already performing the job, he must be briefed carefully about the aims of the study since anxiety is often felt about being watched.

This observation of the job being done is an important part of the information gathering process, as is questioning. The relationship between analyst and job holder must therefore be one of mutual trust or relevant data may be missed. Questions must be framed tactfully and asked of all who are concerned in the execution and background to the job. Other methods of finding out about the job are, firstly, to make use of any existing written material on the job (work study, previous projects, etc.) and by having a go at doing the job oneself. This soon reveals any flaws in the amount of information that is necessary, and also gives one the 'feel' of the job (incoming sensory stimuli which can be translated into action in the teaching phase).

At the end of the process, the analyst will be left with a mass of jumbled information, probably in no set format, which will have to be checked before going any further. Cross checking between superiors and job holders is valuable, since it often reveals anomalies in the perception of the job and what is involved in its successful completion. From this mass of information, the analyst has the basis for the documents that will result from it, the Job Description/Definition and the Job Specification.

Job Description

Sometimes referred to as Job Definition, this document results from Job Analysis and briefly describes what the job is. It can be used for selection, job classification and the organization of work as well as training and is consequently an important tool of management. It is a statement of the purpose, scope, duties and responsibilities of a particular job committed to paper, and one need hardly add, needs constant updating and revision for it to serve its full purpose. The trainer will need to have complete, up-to-date job descriptions for all jobs he is expected to instruct, as this is the document upon which he will base further analysis. Job descriptions can be drawn up by management, specialist training staff or supervision, one good method being to ask the job holder to write his own description, subsequently verifying this with other versions from his seniors. (The exercise is often worth while since it highlights the difference in what actually is done by the job holder and what other people think that he does, a clarification of methods and roles which is a decided help in looking at organizational problems.) Whichever method is used for drawing up the document, emphasis should be placed on the fact that it is a 'living' document, of benefit both to management and staff.

There is one disadvantage with job descriptions, in that demarkation disputes can sometimes arise, when a job holder says 'I'm not doing that, it's not on my job description.' For this

Analysing Jobs

reason, a final phrase 'any other duties as shall be required from time to time as deemed necessary by the Management' is often incorporated. This covers the exigencies of crisis, but of course should not be used unscrupulously by managers (in union firms it would be unlikely anyway!). However, the benefits of people knowing what they are expected to do, of management knowing that all duties are being covered by someone on the staff and finally, the trainer having a basis for analytical instruction far outweigh any defects of the process.

The generally agreed format for drafting Job Descriptions is as follows:

1. JOB TITLE
2. PLACE OF WORK
3. SCOPE AND GENERAL PURPOSE OF THE JOB
   (This is necessary because the title of the job may not give sufficient indication of what the job is. A brief overall view of what the job entails is all that is required, rather than a description of specific duties which comes later.)
4. RESPONSIBLE TO:
   RESPONSIBLE FOR:
   (This refers to the job holder's position in the structure in relation to other job holders, referring to people not things and rank not names, as a rule.)
5. DUTIES/RESPONSIBILITIES
   (List here the major recognizable functions in the job – do not become too involved with tasks; also the emphasis is on duties and not knowledge, i.e. the products of action. Knowledge analysis will come later. Sometimes this is sub-divided into Routine Duties and Occasional Duties.)
6. CONDITIONS/CHARACTERISTICS
   (Any significant influences on the workplace are sometimes included, e.g. hot, dusty atmosphere, but this is exceptional.)

These are the main headings accepted by most trainers as typical of job descriptions. It is sometimes argued that Hours of Work should be included on the document, but this can lead to difficulties especially with part-time jobs when hours are

Analysing Jobs

EXAMPLE: JOB DESCRIPTION

TITLE:	HALL PORTER (DAYS)
PLACE OF WORK:	HOTEL SPLENDIDE
SCOPE/GENERAL PURPOSE:	To attend to the immediate needs of arriving guests and to contribute to their well-being during their stay.
RESPONSIBLE TO:	Head Porter
RESPONSIBLE FOR:	–

DUTIES/RESPONSIBILITIES:
1. Maintain cleanliness of front of house area, including exterior.
2. Check and sort incoming mail and newspapers.
3. Handle guests' luggage on arrival and departure and show guests to correct rooms.
4. Liaise with other departments to ensure co-operation with guests' needs (i.e. garage, laundry, maintenance, valet etc.).
5. Provide up-to-date information for guests on current events, local knowledge, train times etc.
6. Maintain good relations with other porters employed in same department.
7. Acquaintance and compliance with fire regulations and duties during such emergencies.
8. Assist lounge waiters in busy periods.
9. Arrange transport for guests where necessary.

OCCASIONAL DUTIES:
1. Deputize for Head Porter during absence.
2. Assist in arrangements for special functions.
3. Transfer guests' belongings during room change.
4. Such other duties as shall be deemed necessary from time to time by the Management.

Analysing Jobs

variable. However, it would be pointless to be too dogmatic about format since job descriptions are meant to be used, and companies will have their own ideas and policy on layout. One final point; consult the appropriate Industrial Training Board for their ideas on job descriptions, as they can offer useful advice and guidance where such links exist.

Job Specification

You will remember that the job description described what the job is; the job specification specifies what the worker does. In other words it details the knowledge, skills and attitudes necessary for successful completion of the task. The list of tasks will be obtained from a further breakdown of the 'duties' heading on the job description, since the reader will recall our starting premise, that the job consists of several duties (areas of responsibility) and the duty consists of several tasks (specific result elements). So our first step is to make a task list by job description, breaking them down into elements by which a specific result is achieved.

This task list is in itself a valuable aid to training since it becomes the corner stone of the training programme, ensuring that no key result areas are missed during instruction. Sometimes, depending on the complexity of the skills involved, trainers in certain industries will go from the job description to a task list missing out job specification and relying on further analysis at the task level to provide their information. However a complete systematic training scheme must include job specifications since this is the logical time to separate out the knowledge from the skill items in the job.

The format usually adopted is simply to list the tasks (taken from the 'duties' column in the job description) on the left and have headings across the document for knowledge, skills and social skills respectively. If we take the job description already used as an example and itemize the tasks under the first duty the job specification might look like fig. 6.

This example (taken to illustrate the differing headings rather than for its absolute accuracy!) shows some of the factors in deciding what is knowledge, skill or social skill/attitudes.

DUTIES/RESPONSIBILITIES and TASKS	KNOWLEDGE	SKILLS	SOCIAL SKILLS
1. *Maintain cleanliness of front-of-house area, including exterior*			
1.1 Clean windows and glass doors in entrance and foyer	Cleaning materials Stores indent procedure	Window and general glasswork cleaning	Problems of interruption by guests (Diplomacy)
1.2 Clean and polish floor of entrance hall	Parquet floor care Standards required	Use of mechanical cleaner/polisher	
1.3 Cleaning and maintenance of exterior advertisements and menu display cases	Recognition of electrical faults on signs (to inform maintenance) Routine for menu display case especially when to change menus	Procedure for cleaning plastic advertisement signs Use of external menu display cases. How to change menus	Liaison with maintenance department Liaison with receptionist staff
2. *Check and sort incoming mail and newspapers*			
2.1 Check incoming mail	Current guest lists. Staff currently employed.	Sorting mail into appropriate sections. Use of pidgeon-hole sorting system.	Ethics of mail handling (attitudes to)

Fig. 6 Job specification (extract).

Analysing Jobs

The knowledge column is simply factual information the job holder must know to perform the task. The skills column is largely a matter of listing areas of manipulative dexterity, which will improve with practice after they have been demonstrated. Social skills are those involving contact with other people, e.g. the diplomacy needed in handling guests whilst trying to get on with a task or conveying to an already harassed maintenance department the urgent problems of the front of house. Attitudes to work can also be entered here as in the example, where ethics regarding mail will certainly need explanation during training.

Thus it can be seen that the job specification details what the worker does to perform the occupation successfully, and is the second product of the job analysis process, although it should be pointed out that it is possible that all three processes are being carried out simultaneously, as information begins to flow in – fig. 7.

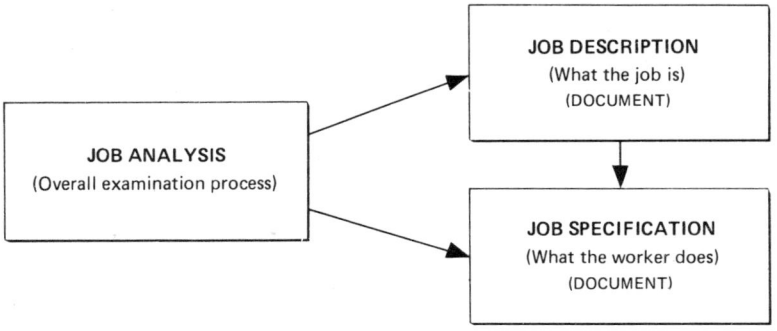

Fig. 7 Job analysis, description and specification.

Chapter Seven

Analysing Tasks

We have arrived at the stage where we know the list of tasks which constitute a particular duty/responsibility and the knowledge, skills and attitudes which are necessary for successful performance. However the trainer will probably need to know much more about each task before he can set up a learning situation for the trainee and there is in existence a series of procedures which will help him to do this.

Analysing Knowledge

The aspects of the task, listed in the Job Specification under the knowledge heading, will need to be described fully so that the trainee is familiar with both the setting and the theoretical aspects of the task. There is no set format for putting these down on paper, but in general they can be divided into two main sections; Company Knowledge and Task Knowledge.

Company Knowledge provides the setting in which the job is carried out. Typical headings which might be included here are company history, company products, manufacturing sequence and processes, departmental structure, organization tree, names of important job holders, company policies (especially with regard to fire, safety and hygiene), wage and salary structure, and social (welfare) facilities. (Note, however, that much of this information may be given at induction, rather than instruction.)

Task Knowledge provides the trainee with the cognitive aspects of his new task, the theory which he will put into practice along with his new skills, the 'head' work necessary for successful performance. Typical headings here for analysis purposes might be:

Analysing Tasks

Names of parts of machines and tools.
Materials used and their origin.
Equipment available.
Work method (operational knowledge).
How work arrives and leaves.
Booking of work.
Quality standards and recognition of faults.
Time allowed.
Team working – who and how many.
Safety as applied to this particular task.
Hygiene requirements for this particular task.
Routine maintenance procedures for fixtures, fittings or equipment.

These task knowledge factors will need to be taught to the trainee at the same time as he is learning the practical skills, so the instructor will need to structure his demonstration session carefully to cover this necessary knowledge, but also to give it at the right time, in the right amount. (Think back to the learning process and the amount of new material that can be absorbed at one time.) Much of the information will in fact be given in the introductory phase of the demonstration, but recalling some of the principles of programme building, it may well be a good idea to have a separate knowledge-type session to vary the trainee's day.

Analysing Skills

The items listed as skills on the Job Specification are more difficult to analyse than the knowledge factors. One major decision the trainer must make is the amount of detail required for the successful tuition of the task, for there are different tools to help him in his analysis depending upon the amount of information required.

Briefly, there are three gradations of detail in analysing skills which will be referred to here as Stage I, Stage II and Stage III.

Stage I analysis
This can be summarized as taking a broad approach to breaking down the task, and is commonly a development of the old

Analysing Tasks

Ministry of Labour 'Training Within Industry' (TWI) format, although with different headings to suit the particular needs of the organization or industry. This is essentially a pragmatic, no nonsense approach to task breakdown which is well within the capacity of even the most junior supervisor. In fairness, it doesn't do much towards analysing the detailed movements of a skill, but at least provides a systematic, step-by-step approach for the trainer, and ensures that the trainer is looking at the task objectively as though he were seeing it for the very first time. As has been said, the headings on simple breakdown sheets are legion, but are usually based on a two-column approach headed 'what is done' and 'how it is done', with a third column for comments or cues in some cases. An example might be that shown in fig. 8.

STAGE I ANALYSIS
(Task breakdown)

Operation: — Striking a match   *Equipment:* — Box of matches

WHAT IS DONE (activity)	HOW IS IT DONE? (key points)	COMMENTS/CUES
1. Pick up box	By holding between Th and forefingers	Correct side up (picture showing)
2. Open box	By pushing tray with Th	Half way only
3. Take out match	With wooden end	Red end away
4. Close box	By pushing tray	Safety!
5. Strike match	By drawing red end on emery paper (away from one)	Fingers close to match head
6. Hold match	With fingers away from flame	Horizontally

Fig. 8   Stage I analysis.

Some of the principles of simple task breakdown (Stage I Analysis) can be seen from this example. The first column starts with a command word and is kept very brief and 'punchy'; the second column starts with an adverb and concisely describes the activity in column one. The third column allows for comments, sensory cues and attention points. It is carried out by watching skilled operators (normally competent workers are best), asking questions if necessary and completing column one, i.e. the basic steps, as a first process. It is advisable to check accuracy by doing the task oneself if possible and checking with supervision or method study to ensure that the procedure is correct. The advantages of this type of analysis are its speed of production, its quick identification of key points and its simplicity, enabling it to be used immediately by any trained instructor. However, it is limited in more complex operations and those where speed may make clear identification in this format unsuitable, i.e. the 'how it is done' column becomes too lengthy and unmanageable.

Stage II analysis
A more detailed form of analysis is the Left Hand/Right Hand form of breakdown, which can be referred to as Stage II Analysis. It is a development of the foregoing, but gives a clearer identification of sequences involving both hands. This is essential in more complex industrial skills, since it enables trainers to identify critical movements and points of difficulty. It has, obviously, headings for left hand and right hand procedures and a column for comments, attention points and cues in the centre. These comments usually employ an arrow pointing to the appropriate hand, where there are differing motions. In fig. 9 we use the same example, though the reader will realize that we would not in fact need different levels of analysis for the same task. The task itself is also simplistic, but almost traditional as an example of analysis!

Stage III analysis
Where tasks are particularly complex, involving very fine sensorimotor skills and where some elements of an operation are extremely critical (e.g. the finger pressure on the wire in

Analysing Tasks

STAGE II ANALYSIS
(Left Hand/Right Hand)

Operation:— Striking a match   Equipment:— Box of matches

LEFT HAND	COMMENTS	RIGHT HAND
1. Pick up box (Th and forefingers)	Correct side up (picture showing)	
2. Hold box	Half way →	Push out tray with Th
3. Hold box	Red end away →	Take out matches Wooden end Th and F_1
4. Hold box	Safety!	Close box Push tray F_3 till shut Hold match Th and F_1
5. Turn box	← Emery paper up	Hold match
6. Hold box	Draw red end away from opening, pressing on emery	Strike match, F_2 close to match head to prevent breakage
7. Hold box	Horizontally → fingers away from flame	Hold match

Fig. 9 Stage II analysis.

coil-winding), the above two methods will not give enough detail for the trainer to be able to identify the learning difficulties. An extension of the left hand/right hand chart to include other sensory cues is vital, and a method often known as 'Skills Analysis' (after W. Douglas Seymour) is used. The format in Stage III Analysis has columns for left hand, right hand, vision, other senses and comments; a five column approach in fact. Another distinct difference from the first two methods is that the breakdown into elements is much finer, in fact the use of any part of the body, for however short a time comprises an element. As in the previous example, activities taking place

Analysing Tasks

simultaneously occupy the same line on the chart. Abbreviations commonly used are Th = thumb, F1, 2, 3, 4, (1st, 2nd, 3rd, 4th fingers) and symbols for the most common hand movements, e.g. R = reach, G = grasp, M = move, AP = apply pressure, RL = release, T = turn, P = position. (This is a convenient form of shorthand based on Methods, Time Measurement – MTM – terminology and is a basis for common usage between work study and training activities.) In addition, it is often useful to make a note of the distance and the angle of reaches and moves.

The column headed 'vision' analyses the part played by the eyes in performing the element, mainly differentiating whether the eyes focus during the operation or merely assist with location. Body movements other than those above are usually written in the comments column. As an example of this form of analysis, we will again use the matchbox in fig. 10, keeping in mind the fact that such levels of discrimination could well be ludicrous for this type of skill. However it will serve to show the difference in procedure between the three stages, hopefully a useful comparison, but the trainer must make careful choice of stages in analysing tasks for effective use of his time. (It is conceivable, for instance, that the analyst may choose to use all three stages of analysis in the same task, depending upon the level of complexity of the element concerned.) It will be noted that the accompanying example needs six lines at Stage III Analysis whereas earlier types have needed only two to reach the same element in the task. However it will be appreciated that the greater detail affords trainers more information upon which to base correct instructional methods, and is often well worth the extra time taken.

To summarize, task analysis is a worth while activity for several reasons:
1. It helps the instructor to view the task as a learner would see it for the first time. This is a valuable asset, since we become blasé and find it difficult to understand their ineptness.
2. The time taken to analyse tasks will be amply repaid by correct, first-time instruction with a saving on fault correction at a later stage.

STAGE III ANALYSIS
(Skills analysis)

Task:— Striking a match Equipment:— Box of matches

LEFT HAND	RIGHT HAND	VISION	OTHER SENSES	COMMENTS
		Eyes to box		
R to box			Kinaesthesis (K) assists	12″ reach
G box Th one side $F_1 F_2$ other		Eyes check correct side (picture upwards)	Kinaesthesis assists →	Light grasp only
M box to central position and regrasp palm uppermost Th LHS $F_1 F_2 F_3$ other side				
Wait, hold box	R to box & P $F_1 F_2 F_3$ on face of box tip of Th on side of tray	Eyes focus on tray end	Touch and K assist	
Wait, hold box	Push out rray with tip of Th	Eyes, check distance of travel	Touch. Th knuckle on end of box indicates safe travel of tray	Approximately half way

Fig. 10 Stage III analysis.

Analysing Tasks

3. The analysis forms the basis for the ensuing instructional material (such as lesson plans or instruction schedules) isolating key points and giving sequential logic to the task.
4. Any particular difficulties can be spotted, and special exercises or other strategies used to cope with them, but, especially, task analysis helps us to decide what are correct break points in stage-by-stage instruction.
5. Where a regular throughput of trainees in quantity is expected (e.g. seasonally) task analysis provides the basis for visual aid design, self-learning techniques and shorter training periods, amply repaying such time as the trainer may have to spend on task analysis.

However task analysis is only a means to an end. Busy trainers will not produce documents which, whilst looking impressive, do not serve their purpose. Experience at analysis (and practice is the best guide), will help the trainer to optimize his analysis time, producing no more nor less detail than correct instruction demands.

Chapter Eight

Preparing to Instruct –
Written Work

The trainer is now in a position to prepare his strategy for instructing his trainees in the knowledge or tasks allocated to him on the training programme, and has already analysed the job material that constitutes the groundwork for his session, though it will not yet be in suitable form for a lesson. The trainer will need to prepare thoroughly three important facets of his task; the written work necessary for presenting the session, the materials and equipment to be used during demonstration and practice (including any visual aids) and finally any instructional material to back up the session such as handouts, etc. The importance of adequate preparation cannot be overstressed, since it is the hallmark of the successful trainer. Many hours of preparation may be necessary for a short session but if it is skimped it will certainly show, not only to the trainees but to people in authority over the instructor. Hence the trainer must set about a systematic preparation in order to provide the trainee with the optimum chance to learn, starting with a clear idea of where he is going.

Instructional Objectives

Pedantic though it may seem, there is a fundamental difference in interpretation between the terms 'aims' and 'objectives', though they are often used indiscriminately by trainers. An aim, in the instructional sense, is often a long-term statement of intent, e.g. to train a new entrant to an accountancy firm in book-keeping; whereas an objective has a short-term learning outcome in the educational sense, which can be measured, e.g. to train the new entrant to prepare a balance. (The two words could almost be said to compare with the words 'job' and 'task',

Preparing to Instruct – Written Work

the former implying a broad statement and the latter the steps to successful achievement.) So an instructional objective can be described as a statement in words of the intended learning outcome of a training session, and furthermore states what the trainee will be able to do as a result of the training.

It is important that the trainer writes his objectives in behavioural terms, i.e. stating the observable activity which will illustrate the gain in ability by the trainee as a result of the session. It should therefore start with an action word (a verb to describe the learning outcome), contain a statement that describes the standard of performance required and a final description of the constraints within which the objective is to be realized. An example might be; 'The intended training outcome is for the trainee to be able to identify standard symbols on a simple circuit diagram of electrical components,' or; 'The trainee will be able to peel potatoes to the standard laid down by the Head Chef using both hand and machine methods as appropriate.' The end result is sometimes termed 'terminal behaviour', i.e. what the trainee actually achieves, whereas the original expectations are referred to as 'criterion behaviour'.

Whatever terminology is used, there are obvious advantages to be gained by describing objectives in behavioural terms:

> The trainer knows terminal behaviour will be observable and can therefore measure the degree of success or otherwise that has been achieved.
>
> The trainee will be motivated to attain the standards of required performance if he knows clearly what is expected of him.
>
> Adequate, objective feedback of a non-emotive kind can be given to the trainee, where performance standards can be accurately and quickly assessed.

Behavioural objectives are more obviously applicable in practical skill-type instructions, but are equally important where knowledge acquisition is the trainer's goal. There is a tendency when drawing up objectives for theory topics to use terms like 'the trainee will understand, the trainee will be acquainted with' etc., but the problem is that there is no clearly demonstrable behaviour that will prove to the trainer (and the trainee) that the objective has been reached. Much better is the use of words like 'list', 'write down', 'explain', 'label', these are observable activities with which to conclude such a knowledge-type session, providing adequate feedback to trainer and trainee alike.

So the trainer should discipline himself to write an objective, whether in knowledge or skill, for each session that he has to conduct. The time taken in formulating such objectives is amply repaid, as indeed is all such preparation, as there is often a subtle difference between the trainee's knowing how a task should be done and his being able to do it after instruction. Drawing up instructional objectives ensures that valid tests can be provided to measure the success of both trainee and trainer.

Session Plans/Instruction Schedules

The next piece of written work that the trainer will need to prepare is a plan for the training session allocated to him. Some trainers instruct directly from the analysis material, but many prefer the extra detail that a separate document offers, and in knowledge instruction it is invariably necessary to re-structure the analysis material into a proper learning experience. Titles for such a document vary from lesson plans and instructor notes to instruction schedules, but for simplicity the document will be referred to here as a session plan.

What details will need to be recorded on such a plan? The first and most obvious necessity is the title of the task or piece of information to be conveyed, followed closely by the objective for the session defined as in the previous paragraphs. The headings will also need to include a list of the materials and equipment to be used (and any prior preparatory work done to them), the time allocated for the session and possibly the location where the session could best be presented.

In planning the actual teaching material into a strategic order, the obvious primary divisions are into beginning, middle and end. The mnemonic, 'Commencement, Core, Conclusion' fits very well and is easily remembered, so we will adopt this as an aid to structuring our time. We also need a columnar approach to indicate key points, the development of the key

Preparing to Instruct – Written Work

point and an indication of any visual aids, display summaries or board work to reinforce the presentation. A pro-forma for such a session plan is illustrated in fig. 11.

Commencement

In completing such a pro-forma, it is necessary to consider some of the fundamental principles of session planning, especially remembering the learning process discussed in earlier chapters. The commencement phase has the objectives of arousing interest, setting the scene for the main subject matter and motivating the students to attend and learn. It is essential that such an introductory stage is carefully planned since it sets the tone for the whole instruction, although it may be short in duration. Some ways of creating interest are:

> Using visual material (models, pictures, the real thing) to set the scene.
>
> Creating impact by shock treatment – a gimmicky but memorable approach if used with care.
>
> Relating material to topical, important events which are relevant to subject matter.
>
> Recounting historical development of subject or relating it to historic episodes.
>
> Using humour; a delicate approach is needed here with the choice of appropriate levels and amounts.
>
> Describing actual personal experience of the topic.

The reader will note that such approaches closely parallel the important factors in the learning process with regard to memorability and ease of acquiring new knowledge. Another factor in the commencement phase is the need to explain the reason for the instruction since it is not always obvious to the trainee just why he needs to know the forthcoming knowledge and skills. The wise trainer will paint the overall picture of the enterprise and exactly where the ensuing session fits in, as young trainees in particular have no overall vision of the relationship between what seems to them mundane detail and the grand design of the concern. Finally in the commencement

Preparing to Instruct — Written Work

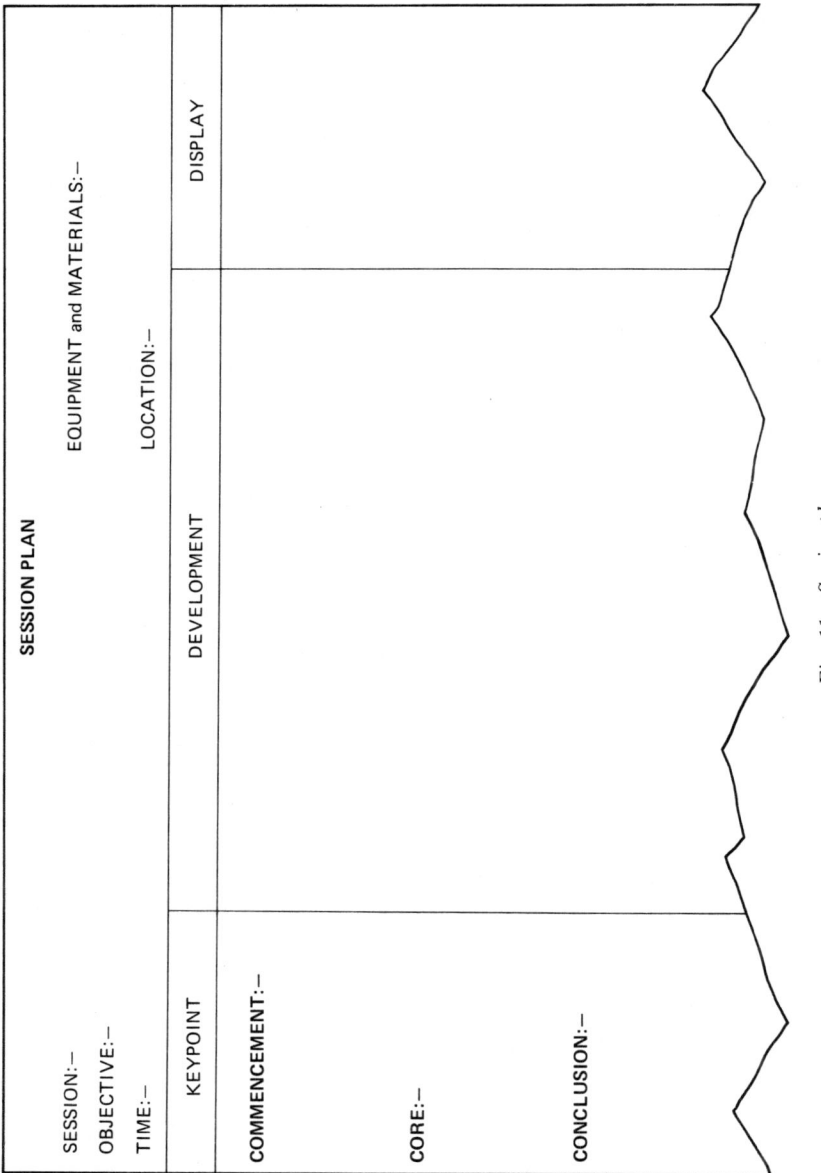

Fig. 11 Session plan.

stage, the trainees must be motivated to learn by pointing out the advantages, especially of learning the new material, particularly those students who require extrinsic motivation. If these trainees can see some gain to themselves in learning they are more inclined to pay attention, so the trainer needs to point out personal incentives such as pay and status, examinations, pride in craftsmanship, increased safety, or any other factors listed in the chapter on motivation that may be appropriate working on his knowledge of the trainees concerned.

Core

Next we come to the main part of the session, the core or development in which all the learning objectives are contained. Certain principles, again based upon the learning process, will help us to structure the core, so that maximum opportunities are afforded the trainee to ingest the new material. The first decision the trainer will make is the choice of teaching method, whether it be lecture, talk, demonstration, discussion or whatever is most suitable to achieve the instructional objective. This choice is so important that a separate chapter on methods of instruction is included later; suffice it to say here that whatever method is chosen, it will need a commencement or introduction on the lines described in the previous paragraphs. For the purposes of discussing the principles of session planning, it is assumed that the trainer has chosen a method in which he provides most of the input, as in a lecture, lesson, talk or demonstration.

The first practical step in planning the core of the session is to decide the degree of importance attached to the information or skill. The material gained from analysis should be categorized into (a) material the trainee must know, (b) material the trainee should know and (c) material the trainee could know. It can be diagrammatically represented as in fig. 12, noting that it resembles a target with the essential information nearest the 'bullseye'.

'Must knows' include all the keypoints thrown up during analysis, without which the task could not be successfully completed, with special emphasis on safety, hygiene and other

Preparing to Instruct — Written Work

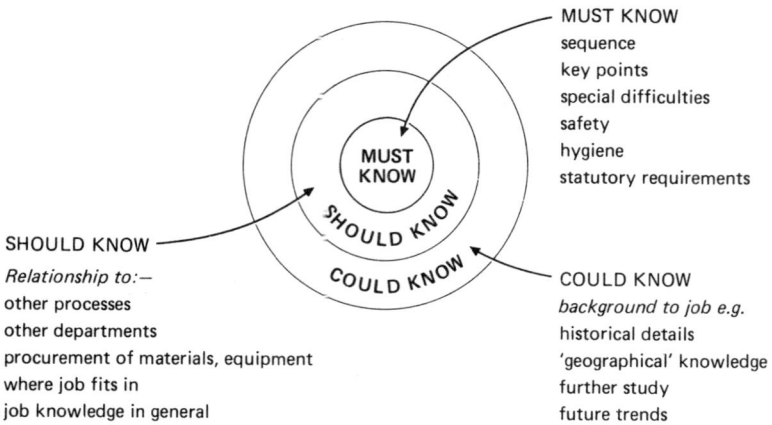

Fig. 12 *Degrees of importance of information.*

statutory factors, as well as stages at which specific learning difficulties have been isolated. These 'must knows' will form the core knowledge and should be emphasized by the trainer during the presentation phase; however the trainer must bear in mind during preparation the target population of trainees that he will be instructing. Factors here include the level of prior knowledge, the educational background and the number of trainees expected, with special consideration of the time available for instruction. This latter factor is, in the writer's opinion, the most likely trap for the novice trainer, since he, almost always, overestimates the amount of material that can be absorbed during one session. The only pointer one can give is to urge the trainer to familiarize himself with the learning process and take a personal interest in discovering the previous knowledge of new trainees; experience provides the rest.

The next factor in planning the core content is the sequence or order in which the material must be presented. Logic is the basis for deciding this order and in most cases it will closely follow the sequence shown up by the analysis. However there are occasions when a particular stage may be taught out of its sequential order for ease of learning. This is particularly true of some complex skills where certain elements have to be practised separately to attain performance standards. (In sewing machining, for instance, guiding the machine may well be taught before threading up, to give the trainee practice.) Indeed, special exercises may be designed at this stage in order to give the trainees expertise at some particularly difficult manipulative skill, entirely separate from the sequential instruction of the task. Another factor in sequence is the principle, mentioned during the learning chapters, of moving from known to unknown material, grafting on new knowledge to that already possessed by the trainee. Again, a thorough knowledge of the trainee and particularly their rate of absorption is important and may well decide the amount of new material at each stage. Other points the reader may recall from the learning chapters are the important ones of moving from simple to complex material at a gradual pace and the whole/part/whole approach to teaching skills.

Participation is a key factor in keeping up the interest and pace of the session during the core phase. Trainers should plan to allow the maximum amount of participation that constraints of time and complexity will allow. (Remember the involvement of all the senses in participative learning.) New methods of instruction, which will be discussed later, have placed heavy emphasis on the trainee learning by experiencing situations ('experiential' learning as it is sometimes called) but even with a large amount of tuition by the trainer, it is possible to bring in the trainee by careful framing of teaching questions (which will be dealt with under instructional technique), by allowing the trainee to practise between steps and by introducing variety in presentation.

The step-by-step approach is particularly useful in teaching manipulative skills and the trainer should decide during the planning phase, exactly where the trainee will actually do something. (Remember the important factors in programme building about length of practice sessions however.) Some trainers use the side-by-side technique with two sets of equipment and materials, the trainer demonstrating and the trainee working along with him. In this technique care has to be taken that the instruction plan shows exactly where demonstration will end and where supervision of trainee's practice takes place, since some serious foul-ups can occur if the trainer and trainee become engrossed in their own product! Finally, the trainer should let it be known what policy he has adopted for note-taking and inform the trainee accordingly; again, more of this in the chapter on instructional technique. To summarize, the core factors are (a) to decide on the 'must knows' and stress them, (b) to teach in a logical sequence, except where special exercise is required in certain complex skills, (c) to proceed from known to unknown, simple to complex, (d) to allow participation wherever possible, since this aids absorption and allows the mind time, necessary during the intake of new knowledge, to process the material into long-term memory, and (e) to refer constantly to the learning process to aid planning, specifically for deciding length of practice time, ('spaced practice is better than massed practice' etc.). And one last plea; in writing up one's teaching notes, make them bold, readable from a standing position and more like memory joggers than copious tomes!

Conclusion

The last phase of the teaching plan will wind up the session, the major purpose being a check that the sessional objectives have been achieved. Consolidation or revision of the main points may take place too, although quite often this review will happen at the end of each stage in the main instruction. In skill-type demonstrations, checking on student performance is a simple matter since he carries out the task to the level of performance required by the trainer. In knowledge type instructions other means of testing have to be adopted, the most obvious being the drafting of testing questions, tests, problems or exercises to assess student intake. The trainer has not completed the learning cycle if he neglects this most vital feedback phase of his instruction, since this is where both trainer and trainee have their performance evaluated. (It is also important to plan time for the trainees to ask questions at this stage, to clear up any little point about which they might not feel completely happy.) Methods of assessment should be as objective as possible and pre-planned pro-formae can be used for short answer tests, true/false tests or multiple choice questionnaires where time permits such an approach. There is certainly a gain for the trainer who uses such test material (apart from the removal of subjectivity) in that it enables a wider range of objectives to be tested and provides the basis for a system of marking and trainee records if desired. Finally the trainer must terminate the session by planning the link with the future, pointing out to the trainees where their future instruction will take them, so it will be necessary to refer to the training programme for this detail.

One last tip; some trainers find it difficult to write the commencement first; if so, leave it until the end, since much valuable material for the introductory phase will naturally reveal itself as the trainer works through the core and conclusion stages.

Chapter Nine

Preparing to Instruct –
Displays and Visual Aids

It will be remembered that the visual sense plays the most important role in perception during learning, so the instructor must carefully prepare the visual material that will support his training session. Much of our ability to remember and recall information is also based on visual presentation; another reason for planning our supporting aids to give maximum impact. Emphasis of the main points in a lesson can be achieved by reinforcing the verbal information with a summary in written form; this form of presentation is often referred to as a display summary, and it is profitable, before going on to analyse the use of visual aids more deeply, to look at some of the major factors in producing such summaries.

Display Summaries

These form the basis of the notes that trainees will take away from the session and as such should possess certain essential requirements. They should be concise, follow the logical development of the lesson and contain all the key points revealed during the analysis phase. They have advantages to the instructor too in that they allow the trainer to check his lesson plan, allow him thinking time and help to provide the variety so necessary in successful presentations. Pre-prepared display summaries allow the trainer to plan the points he intends to emphasize well in advance and can in fact form a framework for the step-by-step illustration of his session. In addition he has the knowledge that his trainees are in possession of correct records of the learning situation when he asks them to take a copy of his display, and of course the physical act of actually writing down the information helps to impress the key points on the trainee's memory. On the other hand, display summaries can be built up progressively as the lesson develops, in conjunction with questioning. This latter method greatly increases participation and there is reward and reinforcement to the trainee when he sees his answer written up on a display summary as a teaching point. It is possible to operate this obvious advantage even with pre-prepared visuals by systematic revealing of the key points, but one is dependent upon the answers to general questions coming in a certain order to fit in with the summary (e.g. on a pre-prepared chart or overhead projector slide). There are ways of getting round this as we shall see later, but most of them are rather involved, thus losing some of the spontaneity of the session. Diagrams, flow charts, tabulated and family tree formats are obviously better pre-prepared, but careful thought should be given to the possibility of starting out with a blank flipchart or blackboard and building up the display as trainees' answers form the framework of the lesson. (Experience in questioning techniques and the confidence of the trainer are also decisive factors.) The use of the display summary will be dealt with more fully under instructional technique, but suffice it to say here that the information written upon the visual must be legible at the back of the training room, be free from spelling mistakes as far as possible and not contain illustrative 'doodles' (which will be incomprehensible to the trainee when slavishly copied and looked up six months later).

Visual Aids

The instructor needs an overall picture of the aids that are available to him. There are many books and pamphlets on the subject and so a practical, subjective view based on experience is all that is offered here. As a general point, it is worth reminding ourselves that visuals are an aid to instruction and can never take the place of the trainer, indeed we can distract our trainees rather than help them if we over-use or abuse visual material. Modern, gimmicky visual aids can give an impression of slickness and appear 'with it', but they can never replace the empathetic journey into knowledge offered by the true teacher.

Preparing to Instruct – Displays and Visual Aids

Since we have been discussing display summaries it might be suitable to start with visual aids which can be used for this purpose.

Boards

Blackboard
The familiar but simple and effective aid that is cheap to produce oneself and easy and economical to use. It is particularly useful for large diagrams, accountancy and columnar work, and the use of multi-coloured chalks will help to produce greater visual impact. With adult students, it tends, unfortunately, to give the 'schoolroom' impression and another disadvantage is the messiness of the chalk itself, but properly used it is still a most effective illustrative medium.

Whiteboard
This board is a more recent development and has a smooth plastic finish, upon which the trainer inscribes with a felt-tip pen. The effect can be more dramatic than blackboard presentation, but beware the use of the wrong type of pen. The ink should be water or spirit type depending upon the recommendations of the manufacturer, and so careful watch must be kept if several trainers use such equipment lest indelible marks be made. (Crayons or pastels are perhaps a safer bet!) One particular advantage of having two types of marker is that when an outline is in permanent use it can be drawn in a spirit-based ink, and water-based felt tips can be used to superimpose additional markings which can be easily cleaned off with a damp sponge. One additional advantage of this type of board is the ability to double up as a projection screen when wiped clean.

Magnetic board
This is another board in common use and, as its name suggests, consists of a steel sheet on which small magnets can be positioned at will. The board is usually surfaced with chalkboard paint and the magnetic material is available in strip and sheet form in contrasting colours (or homemade magnets stuck

to card shapes). It is particularly useful in describing mechanical applications, where movement is critical and has advantages over diagrams and drawings in its mobility.

Flannelboard
This has a board covered with felt, baize or similar cloth as its basis, on to which the material to be displayed is stuck by attaching sandpaper or lint to the reverse side. It is easy to 'do-it-yourself' with an old blanket attached to a board and has advantages in showing built-up sequences or planning working areas.

Pegboard
This is another useful teaching aid, especially for pre-prepared diagrams, models, figures or symbols, an advantage being the ease of attachment of actual objects (the best visual aid of all) by the use of pegs, clips and other fittings.

Plasticboard
The best-known form of this is the 'Plastigraph'. It is made of smooth perspex or similar material and can be used as a teaching aid by pressing on thin, malleable PVC shapes without the need for adhesive (suction holds the two surfaces together when air is excluded). These boards are particularly useful for diagrammatic build-ups in differing colours (as in subjects such as anatomy and physiology) and for planning layouts, where machine shapes etc. can be scale representations in soft PVC.

Projected Aids

These devices in general work by passing light through film or acetate sheeting to project an image on to a suitable screen or matt surface. They have considerable impact, especially when professionally produced film material is used, but could be seen to be 'entertainment' rather than instruction without the full commitment of the trainer to their use as a learning resource.

Slide projectors

These use 35mm film and show one frame at a time, controlled by the trainer both for sequence and speed of operation. Modern slide projectors are available with remote control for ease of commentary and with much improved loading facilities ('carousel' projectors allow slides to be loaded into a circular framework, thus many more slides can be handled). The slides themselves can be produced by the trainer or professionally produced, but the trainer has a real say in the content of a slide presentation if he controls the whole process. *Tape/slide programmes* can be produced in which the slide projector is linked to a tape recorder to give sound commentary either electronically or manually by cueing. The former operates by means of a slide synchronizer, inserting short pulses on the tape track which when passed to the slide projector represent the command 'next slide', and so music and commentary proceed completely in step with the changing and screening of the slides. It can be seen that self-instructional programmes for skill training are a great possibility with this system where the student, using a headset, listens to the instructions, sees illustrations of the work and actually practises the skill at the same time.

Films

Films of the cinematograph type (usually 35mm) are common enough to need no description. As a teaching aid they must be very carefully chosen to illustrate exactly the core of the lesson. Too many trainers mould their own objectives around a proprietory film and lose their way. Many homemade films can be just as good as the professional ones, since what they lose in production skills, they make up for in relevance. It is not as difficult as some might think to produce one's own film. My advice is, if the commercial catalogues do not have exactly the film required and, if the money is available then have a go! In general, I would reiterate the remarks at the beginning of this section, i.e. the film must never be allowed to take the place of adequate instruction since the principal disadvantage of the film is that it must be shown at a pre-determined speed without interruption. Proper introduction, explanation and discussion at the end are essential if films are to be of value. (Needless to say, the trainer must be in total command of the equipment – there is nothing worse than a faulty projector and an impotent trainer! Practise threading up, minor maintenance and film splicing before embarking on film shows, unless a technician is available all the time.) One last tip about film length, remember that a film is a visual aid to memorizing the core features of a session and should therefore not be too long. Ten to twenty minutes is all students can take at one sitting as a rule.

Filmstrips
These enable a film to be shown frame-by-frame, a very useful advantage in skill training. The illustration can be shown for as long as is required and explained and discussed in stages to match the steps in the lesson plan. The major disadvantage is their inability to show movement, but an actual demonstration is sometimes possible by the trainer, or a verbal explanation at the screen using a pointer often gets over this difficulty. Cheaper than movie films and less liable to mechanical failure, this aid is often under-rated as a learning resource, especially since modern filmstrip projectors need no blackout facilities.

Loop projectors
Loop projection is another great boon in teaching skills. The loop projector uses 8mm film wound into a cassette and, as its name suggests, operates by continuous showing of a loop of film by the rear projection method. Loops can be made by the trainer with a home movie kit and loaded into a cassette by specialist firms, or commercial loops can be purchased on a wide range of topics. The screen looks like a television receiver and is ideal for teaching skills to individual students or small groups. The major facility is the constant repetition of points of difficulty, plus the ability to 'freeze' the action with a frame-holding device for closer inspection. As with all rear projection devices it allows trainer and trainee to be in close proximity to the screen without blocking the light source (which works by projecting light through the film, on to a mirror and on to a translucent screen). A costly piece of hardware, but well worth the outlay in circumstances where a large throughput of trainees, in small numbers, is anticipated.

Preparing to Instruct – Displays and Visual Aids

Epidiascopes

The epidiascope projects objects, models, pages of books, diagrams or slides on to a screen. An expensive piece of equipment needing a darkened room, it does not need transparent film in order to illustrate. It is particularly useful for preparing enlargements (i.e. diagrams, drawings, etc.) from an original, but is not common in training departments generally due to cost and size.

Overhead projectors

These are very popular, on the other hand, being portable, reasonable in cost and can be used in normal daylight. It does however need the preparation of clear acetate 'transparencies' since the light source, by means of a lens system, projects the images inscribed on the acetate through an overhead mirror to a large screen. The general method of operation is to place the overhead projector alongside the trainer, who places his pre-prepared acetate sheet on to a horizontal glass plate, which is then projected on to the aforementioned screen behind him. The advantage here is that the trainer can always face his group unlike board work, and can even write in longhand on an acetate roll, rather than use pre-prepared sheets, if he so wishes. It has a more 'with-it' image than board work, being acceptable to adult students particularly in supervisory and managerial training. It is clean to use, has a vast range of illustrative possibilities particularly when overlays of different colours are superimposed upon one another, and displays can be retained indefinitely if spirit-based pens are used in preparation. It has a number of advantages in the learning process, if one recalls the theoretical principles outlined in earlier chapters, in that it helps in maintaining interest, has impact and aids the organizational aspects of learning since it encourages hierarchical presentation of material because of the small surface area. It allows maximum eye contact and, provided the major principles of OHP transparency design (ABC – Accurate, Brief and Clear), are adhered to is an excellent, participative aid. Its disadvantages are costs (compared to boards) since even after the initial outlay, consumables such as acetate and frames can accumulate quite a large debit on the training budget (particularly if OHP use is suddenly considered 'vogueish' by trainers and a craze is started!). Other disadvantages, to be reconciled with its obvious student-centred appeal, result from its sheer mechanical construction. It needs a cooling fan, which is intrusive, it can blow a bulb at the most inconvenient time and it needs appropriate electrical supply and connection. (NB, most portable OHPs need to cool off before being moved.) The upper lens intrudes into the line of vision of some students however carefully placed and an over enthusiastic trainer constantly whipping acetates on and off the machine can cause the student to 'switch off'. (The number of transparencies shown has to be carefully thought out.) However, there is no doubt that for sheer visual stimulation, the OHP deserves its place as the visual aid which has made most impact in the last two decades, and all trainers are duty bound to make themselves familiar with it. There is incidentally an attachment for the machine which allows $3\frac{3}{4}$in. slides to be projected in daylight (or 2in. slides of 35mm film less well) and a useful adaptation is the facility of demonstrating working models in transparent or translucent plastic, much used in engineering training, by positioning the models on the glass screen.

Charts

Flipcharts
Another visual aid that has had quite large sales to trainers in recent years is the flipchart, consisting of sheets of paper varying in weight and price from newsprint to cartridge paper clamped to an easel or whiteboard. The instructor inscribes upon the paper in felt-tip pen, crayon, chalk or poster paints, either in advance of the session for a pre-prepared set of aids or in situ as a progressively built-up display summary during a training session. The advantage of the former is that a flipchart is preferable to board work where permanency is required and pre-prepared charts can be stored and used over and over again. The latter method of usage enables the trainer to give immediacy to his session and encourages participation. It is clean, cheap if newsprint is used (or if thicker paper is written on both sides) and has the inestimable propensity of enabling

Preparing to Instruct – Displays and Visual Aids

the trainer to cover the previous chart, without displaying the next, by the use of blank sheets – a great help in staging a knowledge-type session. Its disadvantages are its size (usually the sheets are bought in smallish, pre-punched tablets to match the easel) especially for work involving figures or large diagrams, and the inability to correct mistakes easily. However most flipcharts are extremely portable and look 'modern' as opposed to a chalkboard, a useful sideline being the ability to clamp or stick diagrams or pictures when it is not actually being written on.

Wall charts
These consist of sheets of cartridge or similar paper, linen or other durable material which are simply attached to a wall by a variety of methods (tape, plastic, rubber etc.). Usually pre-prepared by commercial firms or by the trainer himself, a high degree of presentation can be achieved with good design. Wall charts can be a great help to the student during the process of memorization and recall, aiding the trainee to organize his incoming information and helping him through the 'rehearsal buffer' from short- to long-term memory. The principles are the same as in all visual material – accurate, brief, clear, with no clutter, good use of colour and with as much impact as possible. Some trainers surround the training area with wall charts, often a good idea *after* the information has been taught as an *aide memoire*, but beware of overloading the receptor processes by having too much new material on view. A good ploy is to use the board to help with simple concepts that are more fully described on a wall chart, as in mechanical diagrams of some complexity.

Flap sequences
These are somewhat similar where a series of charts are bound together but shown in succession to illustrate stages in a process or mechanism. In essence it is rather like a frame-by-frame slide show but can illustrate greater detail in drawings than photographs, especially when dealing with internal processes that the camera cannot see.

Televisual Aids

The major instructional use of television is the well-known *Closed Circuit Television* (CCTV) system. The camera, controlled through monitoring devices, gives a display on a television receiver. Colour video cameras will now produce colour pictures and, in conjunction with a video tape recorder (VTR), permanent recordings can be made on videocassettes. The scope of such a system is obviously enormous, since videotapes can be produced for a huge range of instructional purposes locally, or commercial tapes purchased from an increasingly large selection using only a playback facility. Cost is the major consideration, plus the necessity for thorough technical training for the operator/technician but the potential, particularly in skills training, amply repays the expenditure where the target population of trainees is high. The ability to give almost instant feedback for fault correction and checking is very important, and on the recording there is no subjective argument. It is also extremely useful in social skills training, where role play can be recorded and the trainees use the VTR for self-criticism and analysis (NB, this is invaluable for the training of trainers). Without VTR facilities, CCTV has been used for many years to enable one trainer to address trainees in several different locations, and to show inaccessible or potentially hazardous views to groups of trainees. One disadvantage, apart from the cost and the necessity for fault-free technical support, is the reluctance of some trainees to appear before the television cameras. Experienced trainers know that the student will soon lose all consciousness of the camera in the concentration upon the task, but it is sometimes extremely difficult to convince the reluctant, introvert trainee that this is so (and, indeed, it may be traumatic for some very shy people at first). However, the videotape recording is invaluable for communications skills at all levels of the company, from selection interviewing to reception training, provided the playback is conducted by an experienced, empathetic trainer.

Models

These are often next best to the real thing, especially if they are to scale, although they do not necessarily give the correct impression of size. However they do have the undoubted major advantage of being three-dimensional, which no other aid has. Expense and time in construction are disadvantages, but for realism it is often worth this expenditure, especially since they can be sectionalized to show principles or constructed with moving parts. It need hardly be stated that the simulation must be as accurate as possible to be of real value, so quite considerable expertise is needed to construct models to specification, which may well warrant expert outside help or craftsmen employed as technicians for the training department. This, however, could well be an investment since a model is a permanent, tangible and satisfying form of visual aid, which can be used over and over again.

On-job Aids

Quite often aids can be extemporized on the job using materials and fittings to hand. The trainer in the workplace can be creative in improvising illustrative material from his immediate surroundings, or by using tiled walls or similar washable surfaces as displays. In general it is better to pre-plan the use of visual aids prior to the session, but quite often there is some little point that the trainee will not understand, which the trainer could not have foreseen. It is then that the 'instant' visual aid made from cardboard boxes or chalked on the side of a machine can bring enlightenment. On-job trainers should always carry around a piece of chalk, a chinagraph pencil and a water-based felt-tip pen. Spare paper and a folder are essential too, for the immediate illustration of some point, and also for photographs and diagrams which need to be carried around. (A folder can also be used as a temporary support for pictures and drawings if opened out and used like an easel.) Pieces of board are nearly always available in an industrial setting and these too may be excellent supports for paper illustrations pinned or stuck to them in an emergency. The lesson is, the instructor must be creative and think on his feet in an instructional setting, as instant aids and models can be found all around if one gets used to looking.

To sum up, visual aids are tools in the hands of the trainer. They can never be a replacement for the good instructor, even with 'teaching machines' (which will be discussed later under programmed learning). It is important to be able to choose the correct aid for the job, and it is hoped that the foregoing will act as a guide to their use. Too many training schemes still stick to the 'chalk and talk' of lecture and blackboard, but this is changing with growing awareness of the ways in which people learn. Visual aids need not be expensive to be effective and the ingenuity of the trainer can be brought to bear in the visual field. One general point, it is advisable to display the visual aid at the relevant point in the session and then remove it, since it could serve as a distraction if left up longer than necessary. (The use of the aid should always be indicated in the instruction schedule/lesson plan under a separate column and it is often a good idea to indicate when to remove the aid in the same way.) Finally, it is always wise, not only to plan the timing and choice of an aid, but to rehearse its use carefully before the actual session, particularly with mechanical or electrical equipment. A rehearsal period prior to the session can iron out snags, give the trainer time to reflect quietly on his strategies and increase his confidence during the real thing, helping him to cope with the unexpected emergencies that can 'throw' the unprepared instructor.

Chapter Ten

Choosing the Right Method –
Imparting Knowledge and Changing Attitudes

In terms of sequence, the trainer must choose which method of instruction he is going to adopt as soon as he knows his instructional objective. His chosen strategy will depend upon several factors – the learning process required, whether it be information, skills or attitude changing, the size of his group, their previous knowledge, their age range and background, the facilities available to him and the amount of money budgeted, being just some of them. Moreover, the trainer will need to know which method of instruction will achieve his objectives and have a good overall picture of the range of strategies open to him. To further this, there follows a discussion on the major ways in which the trainer can impart knowledge and change attitudes, with comments on the usefulness of each method.

The Lecture

This is traditionally the most formal method of instruction, and usually consists of verbal explanation or description of the subject matter, with or without illustration. Usually during lectures, the trainee is passive, listening and watching in silence without interruption in the form of questions or discussion. It is often lengthy in duration, without trainee participation, questions being answered in a separate section at the end, or in separate tutorials at a later date. It has been in use for centuries, and is the preferred learning style to this day in many higher institutions and state organizations.

As a strategy it has many advantages for the trainer and several purposes, including:

It can be used to give an overall view of the subject matter as an introduction, the detail being filled in later (often by a different method).

The presentation of new techniques and procedures, of which the trainees can have no previous knowledge.

The stimulation of interest in a new direction, line of thought or development.

Teaching complex information, which can be precisely worked out beforehand even to the exact word.

The most obvious application is where there are large numbers of trainees needing information, where participation is not possible because of the sheer volume of people. The timing can be worked out exactly and entered in the lesson plan with sure knowledge that the trainer will in fact cover the ground he intended to. This is rarely so in any other method of instruction. (Statistics which may help this planning process are that the average trainer will speak at one hundred words per minute and the average A4 double-spaced typewritten sheet has 350 words per page.) The principles of planning a lecture were covered in the earlier chapter on lesson design, but without trainee questioning or discussion.

Some of the disadvantages of the lecture as a learning experience are obvious. The lack of involvement of the trainee leaves the trainer without feedback on the trainee's rate of assimilation of the material. Unless the whole of the presentation from beginning to end is fully understood and assimilated, the sequence and sense will be lost, since only questioning at the end will provide enlightenment and that may be too late. The problem is of course that not enough of the senses are employed in this method of instruction and thus perception is affected.

To counter this problem *seminars* are sometimes arranged after a lecture. In a seminar one member has prepared an opening paper based upon the previous lecture, and a group discussion ensues. This gives an opportunity for clarification, development of concepts and exchange of views and ideas on the subject matter. Seminars need not, of course, follow a lecture but be based upon an agreed subject, known in advance to all the members, who can acquaint themselves with it and come prepared to make an informed contribution. The opening statement should not occupy more than ¼–⅕th of the time available, and the trainer should stay in the background so that the trainees can learn to express themselves, discuss and classify their own ideas on the topic. The maximum number of participants should not exceed twenty in any one group, and a seminar can be followed by tutorials.

Tutorials are usually one-to-one or one-to-two-or-three at the maximum in trainer/trainee ratio. Tutorials are the final link in the lecture, seminar chain (fig. 13) when individual problems are ironed out or the student prepares some work for the trainer to criticize constructively. It is an almost essential feature of the lecture system, since it provides the evaluation phase in this rather remote form of tuition, both for lecturer and student.

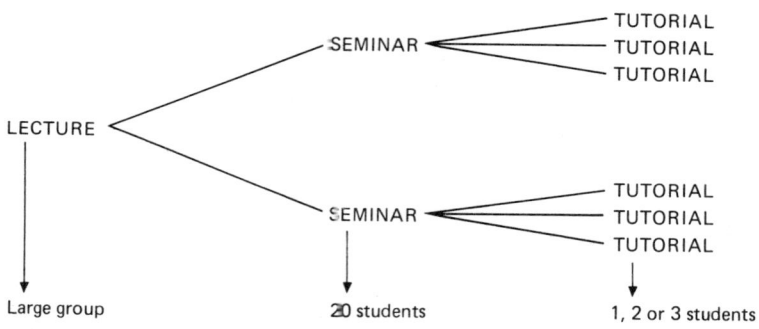

Fig. 13 Relationship of tutorials to lectures.

Although lectures are becoming less popular as a form of learning design, they still have great relevance, particularly in large companies, on topics like new research, product development or new legislation (especially in health, safety and hygiene areas) and are also much used in the induction process where large numbers of trainees are taken on simultaneously.

Talks/Lessons

Talks and lessons incorporate a variety of techniques, but their chief difference from a lecture is in the amount of participation allowed by the trainer. This format is suitable for knowledge-type sessions to groups of not more than twenty trainees and preferably twelve to eighteen, since participation is difficult to handle above such numbers. The lesson is classically planned in the commencement, core, conclusion style, with the trainee involvement generally in the core and conclusion phases. The trainer will encourage participation by questioning, being questioned and discussion in the core phase and by some form of testing in the conclusion phase. There will also be visual aids to help to display summaries, some form of note taking and a little direction from the trainer who will allow interruptions for clarification and other points. It is more of a two-way dialogue than a lecture with 50:50 or 60:40 ratio of trainer/trainee input. The student uses more senses in his learning process and the trainer has more awareness of student needs, so it should be a more efficient learning vehicle than the lecture.

However there are, needless to say, some snags. The timing of a lesson is more difficult to gauge, since the amount of trainee participation is impossible to assess first time around and, indeed, differs from group to group. In some groups, nothing may come back in the form of questioning or reaction from the trainees, whilst other groups will argue and furiously debate every teaching point. Also the trainer must have good interactive skills to handle a participative group successfully, unlike the straight lecturer, being able to draw out the shy and control the talkative, but, in return, he will have a much more accurate idea of the trainee's ability. Whether it be lesson or lecture, a general rule of thumb guide to input for the trainer is to limit his concepts to not more than four per hour (expressed diagrammatically in fig. 14).

This is difficult to achieve, but is the key to successful knowledge-type instruction. If nothing much comes back from the trainees, the instructor will tend to rush through his material until it becomes rather like a lecture, and he will fail to achieve his instructional objective. If his groups are over-

Choosing the Right Method – Knowledge and Attitudes

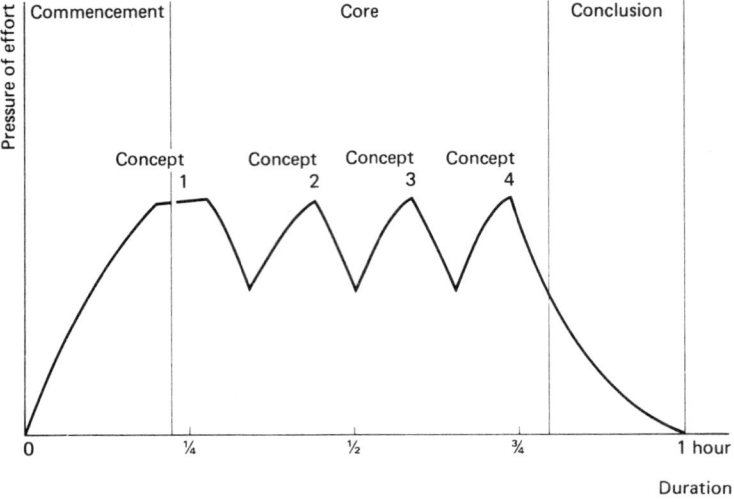

Fig. 14   Lesson structure.

talkative, he again may fail since he cannot introduce sufficient concepts in his allotted time span. Careful planning, experience and the ability to handle his group with empathy and with sensitive 'antennae' are the only ways to overcome the dangers of the participative talk or lesson. It is important to test objectively the amount of learning that has taken place during the core phase by some means (discussed in the chapter on lesson planning) before terminating the session, since this will provide the information for future talks of lessons on the receptivity of the individual student, on the success of the lesson and on the amount of remedial teaching that may be necessary in the future.

Discussion Groups

One of the most effective means of inducing attitudes and developing social skills is the group discussion. The trainer acts in a limited way as a scene setter, referee or catalyst, getting his students to put into words their feelings, ideas and opinions on the topic in question. There are several different kinds of discussion groups depending upon the instructional objective. The *controlled* discussion group has a set topic and the trainer exercises control so that the group ends with a set conclusion. This teaches by exchange of information where prior knowledge of core facts is assumed but where interpretation may be a matter of opinion. The *associative* group discussion uses a specific topic, but the trainees arrive at their own conclusions, although the trainer does not allow too much deviation and would probably summarize at the end. The *free* discussion has no set topic and teaches discussion methods mainly (debate, argument, development of logic, confidence in expression etc.) as an end in itself, the conclusion not being paramount.

Trainees are influenced by one another in peer groups and are much more likely to change attitudes during group discussion than if they were told that their attitude should be changed by their boss. It is also a valuable means of obtaining feedback for the instructor, particularly when the practical applications of some new knowledge are being discussed, since he can gather information about the way in which the group have grasped important concepts. Finally it helps the trainer to assess the verbal skills, the level of motivation and some aspects of personality in his group. Needless to say, there are some disadvantages in running group discussions. The balance of the group needs careful analysis if the dynamics are to be correct, with the right proportions of strong contributors, shy introverts, logical thinkers and happy followers. This is not a treatise on group psychology, but trainers who make a feature of this type of work could well make a study of groups if they are to become good interactive trainers. (More will be said about running groups under instructional technique, by the way, but group psychology in depth is outside the scope of this book.) Numbers too are important in group discussion, with maximum interaction occurring between five and eight people; certainly anything over twelve should be split into two groups, although this does present chairmanship difficulties.

The role of the trainer is important in *controlled* group discussions where trainees may stray from the subject or fail to discuss it fully, or may display entrenched attitudes and futile personality conflicts. Again, more of this later in the chapter on instructional technique. Suffice it to say here that the instructional objective must be carefully worked out to include one or more of the following applications:

> Influencing colleagues' attitudes.
> Inducing attitudes to the organization and its customers.
> Relating practice to principles.
> Problem solving.
> Analysis of existing procedures and practices and 'brainstorming' solutions.

Role-play

This is a primary means of teaching social skills and inducing preferred attitudes. The trainees are asked to enact a role which will be the same, or as near to, their working role, but in the protected invironment of the training scene. It is often linked to some prior input such as lectures, talks or conferences and is used as an opportunity for the trainees to put into practice some of the skills, especially the communication and human relations skills, that have been discussed. It is valuable as a means of giving the trainee an insight into his own behaviour and its effect upon other people, and is especially valuable when linked to some objective feedback system like CCTV videorecordings.

Typically, two or more trainees will role-play a situation in front of the rest of the group. The scenario is usually unscripted, but full briefing of the role and the setting is given by the trainer, usually without rehearsal. The trainees are allowed to plan their actions, prior to a spontaneous performance before the group. Typical situations where role play can be used effectively are instructor training, interviewing (grievance, selection, disciplinary), counselling, appraisal, sales training and customer relations. It is especially recommended for service industries, where such a lot depends upon social skill and yet where little effort seems to be made in some concerns to develop natural abilities in this field.

The advantages of role play are:

> It has high interest and involvement for the trainees.

There is almost immediate knowledge of results from the objective appraisal of the spectators and tutor.

It increases sensitivity to other people's points of view, since it is relatively easy in most role-play situations to reverse roles (i.e. the interviewer becomes the interviewee).

The trainer can appraise fairly accurately (by the success or otherwise of the role playing) how well his instruction has been absorbed, and give a fair assessment of his trainees' likely work performance after some practice at this interactive technique.

The trainees get the feel of the real-life pressures of the working situation and yet are protected. This results almost invariably in an increase in self confidence on the part of the trainee.

Of course, it is a technique not without its dangers. Trainees may become embarrassed, especially those of a shy, introvert nature, unused to such situations. Most will suffer from initial nervousness, which will have to be counteracted by empathetic help and encouragement from the instructor. On the other hand, the extrovert can 'overact' and regard the session as a 'bit of a lark' not to be taken too seriously. (From experience the best way of dealing with the latter situation is to allow the group to exercise its own discipline upon the deviant member.) However, in spite of these drawbacks, it remains one of the most effective teaching media for face-to-face situations, i.e. where people interact socially in the work situation, and, with a practised trainer, can really help with self analysis and improvement in attitudes.

Case Study

Another excellent means of promoting self awareness, developing empathy towards other people's points of view and gaining knowledge by doing is the case study. Widely used in teaching supervisory and management techniques (such as personnel, industrial relations, marketing, business law and production policy), it consists of a historical report of a set of circumstances or an event, with all the relevant material and background for the trainees to be able to examine the case, solve problems maybe or to derive useful generalizations and principles. Like role play and discussion groups, it is a highly active method of training, with maximum involvement of all the senses and student interest is usually high, especially if the case history is based upon a series of actual events.

The real advantages of this approach are in attitude formation and change. It is extremely useful for illustrating important principles about business life, e.g. the possibility of several solutions to a problem and the consequent reduction of narrow-mindedness, the frustration of situations in which no-one tells people what to do, and the advantages of integrating knowledge obtained from a number of foundation disciplines, etc. Again it is free from the actual working pressures and helps to form the ability to take a long, cool look at situations that have occurred in real life. Needless to say, the studies must be realistic, the briefing and concluding plenary sessions properly conducted by the trainer and careful selection for balance be made in the groups working together upon the case, or trainees may get the wrong impression of the real work situation. Bonuses from the case study come when students have to learn to defend their proposals, often in the face of keen criticism from other groups. They also learn to weld dissimilar disciplines such as engineering and salesmanship and soon appreciate that there is no single answer to a problem and no progress without compromise in many areas.

The foregoing methods of instruction offer a choice in imparting knowledge and changing attitudes. They are just some of the major techniques used in this area; the trainer must take into account the advantages and disadvantages of each approach when examining his instructional objective. More techniques in which the trainer plays a completely passive role in the instructional process are described in the chapter on experimental and programmed learning.

Chapter Eleven

Choosing the Right Method –
Imparting Skills

Demonstration and Practice

The usual way of imparting skill is by an experienced trainer performing the working activity, at pre-determined speeds, telling the trainee how to do the task, showing the trainee the movements involved and coaching the trainee whilst he practises. This we tend to call demonstration, though in fact each of these parts could be a complete session in itself. Often the task is broken down into distinct stages, each one being practised separately (the chapter on the learning process states the advantages of this approach). The whole skill is thus built up from step-by-step instruction. It will be noted that this technique merely teaches psychomotor dexterity and any resultant principles or theory must be taught by one of the methods outlined in the previous chapter.

It is successful because it uses all of the learner's senses, if properly planned and organized. Visual material, discussion, question and answer techniques will all provide important learning stimuli to back up the demonstration. Needless to say, an essential aspect of this technique from the trainer's point of view is the need for prior rehearsal of the skill, often to a pre-determined speed and quality standard. Failure to achieve this sort of target often results in lack of credibility since the trainee does not believe the targets are really possible. A smooth performance during demonstration increases confidence on both sides of the learning relationship, so it is well worthwhile to get in some practice prior to the event! The dictionary definition of 'to demonstrate' is 'to make manifest', therefore it is essential that demonstrations as far as possible use the actual equipment in the real workplace, i.e. on-the-job

Choosing the Right Method – Imparting Skills

training, if skills are being taught. (Another application of demonstration is to illustrate a principle during a knowledge-type session but this may or may not teach a skill afterwards.) Alternately, in off-job training situations, realistic and accurate reconstructions of the working environment are desirable, if the trainee is to practise in something like real conditions. However, some on-job demonstrations are disorganized and haphazard due to distraction, lack of instructional technique or the pressure of work tending to denigrate principles and theory in favour of immediate production needs.

Thus demonstrations need careful, strategic build-up by a competent trainer to be really successful, and considerable coaching skills during the resultant practice by the trainee if they are to reach experienced worker standard within the allotted time span. A typical skill-type session based upon the demonstration and practice technique might look like this:

> Commencement.
> Check (positioning of trainees, everything ready).
> Demonstrate silently at usual speed for task.
> Demonstrate the task again, this time with verbal explanation, one stage at a time.
> Discussion, question and answer, clarification.
> Demonstration by trainees individually with trainer correcting faults.
> Trainees dispersing to practise.
> Supervised practice by trainees, trainer acting as coach.

Simulation

Equipment or techniques that duplicate actual conditions as closely as possible, yet in an off-job situation, are known as simulators. The classic examples of simulation are the Link trainers used to train pilots during World War Two and the modern mock-ups of the flight deck which are used to train commercial airline pilots. Simulation is most necessary where on-job practice would result in serious injury, or expensive error, if the trainee were to make his normal quota of mistakes. Usually trainee interest is extremely high in simulation exercises, since it most closely follows actual job conditions, and consequently the trainer has few motivational problems. However the cost of simulators is high as a rule, since much research and development is necessary to produce the often complex equipment. It is obviously most important that the simulation closely follows normal practice and is constantly updated by operational data as actual working conditions change, and also that the standard of instruction is high.

Business and Management Games

Not all simulation is to do with psychomotor skills, since it is the core of Business and Management Games, essential in developing supervisory and managerial skills. In this simulated environment, trainees are presented with information about a concern – its markets, products, work force, financial position etc. – and the trainees assume given management roles usually in groups. These groups then run the company; making decisions, dealing with people and taking action. Often the results of the game are computerized, comparing the groups' actions to a pre-determined model of the likely outcome. Feedback is prompt, so that analysis of the trainee's actions and their likely effects is quickly forthcoming. The simulation of the real-life situation aids the transfer of learning from classroom to boardroom, and again is necessary since managers applying theoretical principles to actual situations without practice could end up in severe financial straits or cause endless labour relations problems. The main difficulty, of course, is in assessing the probable results of a trainee's actions, since the learning outcome for the trainee will be affected if he feels the assessment is not realistic, but if credibility in this crucial aspect is achieved, business games can help in developing many facets of a manager's role. Simulation is a valuable tool in assessing trainees' likely performance on the job and providing the trainer with a good idea of the potential of individual trainees.

In-tray Exercises

Another form of simulation, used in the skill training of desk workers at all levels in the company hierarchy, is the In-tray. Trainees are given a series of letters, papers, memos and files similar to the assortment they would get in a normal day's work. They are then asked to take action on each piece of material, giving their reasoning for each decision, and the results are given as feedback to the trainer. Not only does this method teach skills of organization, communication, paper handling and recognition, it also helps with attitude formation on such things as judgement of priorities, panic decisions, attitudes to superiors and juniors, complaint procedures etc. It has the usual pros and cons of simulations, i.e. the need to follow closely real-life practices and pressures to be credible and the need for empathetic feedback by the trainer which should build confidence rather than sap it. However, clerical and desk skills in general seem to develop quickly by this method, especially where real bits of material from a real in-tray have been incorporated into the session.

Exercises

These are really means of developing skills rather than imparting them, but are included here because they often follow closely on a demonstration, or may occur as a test of existing skill prior to training. In this method of instruction, trainees are asked to undertake a task leading to a specific result, following well-defined lines. The trainer briefs the individual or group, determining the line of activity the trainee will take and marks or assesses the results of their actions.

To some extent, during exercises, the trainees are on their own; more so than when being supervised during initial practice of the skills concerned. The trainer often acts only as observer during exercises, not as coach, since it is a 'half-way house' to the real thing. A highly active form of learning, exercises are suitable for any situation where the trainees have to put into practice skills which are partially developed, and relate them to their future jobs, following a pattern or formula laid down by the trainer. Best results are gained from graded exercises which allow trainees to feel the result is reasonably attainable, not too easy nor too difficult, or the trainees will experience frustration and lose confidence. A splendid form of assessment, exercises are often used nowadays instead of formal tests, to gauge students' progress.

Other methods of skill development will be discussed in the next chapter on self-learning techniques. The foregoing descriptions will, it is hoped, help the trainer to choose appropriate strategies for teaching psychomotor skills. Skills involved in supervision and management will be dealt with under a separate heading later in the book.

Chapter Twelve

Do-It-Yourself Learning –
Programmed and Experiential Instruction

Certain training techniques require very little didactic input from the instructor. The learning situation is devised so that the trainee can control his own instructional process, with the majority of the trainer's effort being expended in the design phase. This has some advantages for the trainee in that (a) he can learn at his own pace (b) there is a great deal of participation by the trainee in his own learning process, therefore he is using all the senses, and (c) the motivational aspect is high as a result.

Programmed Instruction

This is a fairly recent development in the field, dating back to the fifties. It is based on Skinner's work on operant conditioning and concentrates on changes in behaviour, and so is therefore a true learning experience. However the programme is the critical factor, in which the instructional objective is expressed as initial behaviour and terminal behaviour, bridged by four or five logical steps between key points. The basic unit of a programme is called a frame since it represents material that is exposed at one time, either in a book, manual or so called 'teaching machine' (more of which later). The frame contains a statement, a question or a problem, to which the trainee makes a response. Sometimes the frames review old material or consolidate, but mostly they introduce new material a little at a time. The student may be required to answer a question, to write a solution or to make a choice from multiple answers, and is given immediate feedback.

The two major formats used in programming are the linear programme and the branching programme. The linear programme, as its name suggests, proceeds in a straight line from initial behaviour to terminal behaviour, with the student moving on from frame to frame regardless of whether his response was correct or not. In the branching programme, the learner is given alternatives from which to select and depending upon his answer, travels down one branch or another. If he chooses incorrectly, his error will be pointed out to him and he is referred to an earlier step to avoid making the error again. If he chooses correctly, he moves ahead and may be given the opportunity to jump a few frames if he shows real insight.

From the foregoing, it will be appreciated that linear programmes can be presented in an unsophisticated format such as a book (with the answers covered over on one side by a sliding strip). The branching programme on the other hand needs an automated device if it is complex, and these are often termed 'teaching machines'. These devices display the frame on a small screen and choices are made by means of buttons or some other mechanism. In some cases computers may assist the mechanism to decide from moment to moment what should be done in instructional sequence. (Of course, many effective programmes are a combination of linear and branching progressions depending upon the complexity of the stage.)

The trainer's role is in programme writing which, in every sense, is an art. It can be a costly, time consuming and frustrating experience, since most programmes are produced by pilot testing on a pragmatic, 'suck-it and see' approach, with constant review and revision. Little research has been done to prescribe a set of rules for developing successful programmes, but designing key frames which have four or five logical steps between them, progressing in difficulty is a useful approach. The terminal step is the desired learning outcome, so one starts from this; then goes back to step one, which should be easily answerable. The intermediate steps should lead logically through the process, an important factor seeming to be the penultimate step which should not 'prompt' the final answer. Consider fig. 15, an example taken from a supervisor's programme outlining the relationship between management and people.

The difficulties of getting the required response are obvious,

Do-it-Yourself Learning

QUESTION	RESPONSE
1. How do you know when a task has been 'managed'?	It gets done
2. Does a manager get things done by himself?	No
3. Who does things for him?	Other people
4. How would you define management?	Getting things done through other people

Fig. 15   Step-type programme.

especially in question one, which is wide open to interpretations other than the one wanted. Quite a developed sense of inferential logic is required of the trainee for there to be a successful learning outcome, yet the effectiveness of the approach can be sensed from the example. Again it emphasizes the process of successive revisions and improvement by pilot testing on groups of trainees and rewriting the programme to take care of the difficulties they experience.

To conclude, another mention of the advantages of programmed instruction which will be offset against the costs of programme writing (or buying commercial programmes) and any hardware.

> The learners experience instant information feedback; knowledge of results is critical for learning.
> Active participation of trainees all the time is guaranteed.
> Students progress at their own pace.
> Programmed instruction can take place anywhere.
> The trainer is freed for other tasks.

Algorithms

These are similar to programmed instructions in that they represent a logically ordered sequence of rules, questions or instructions, 'branched' to allow a variety of possible responses, but exhibited as a complete diagram rather than frame by

Do-it-Yourself Learning

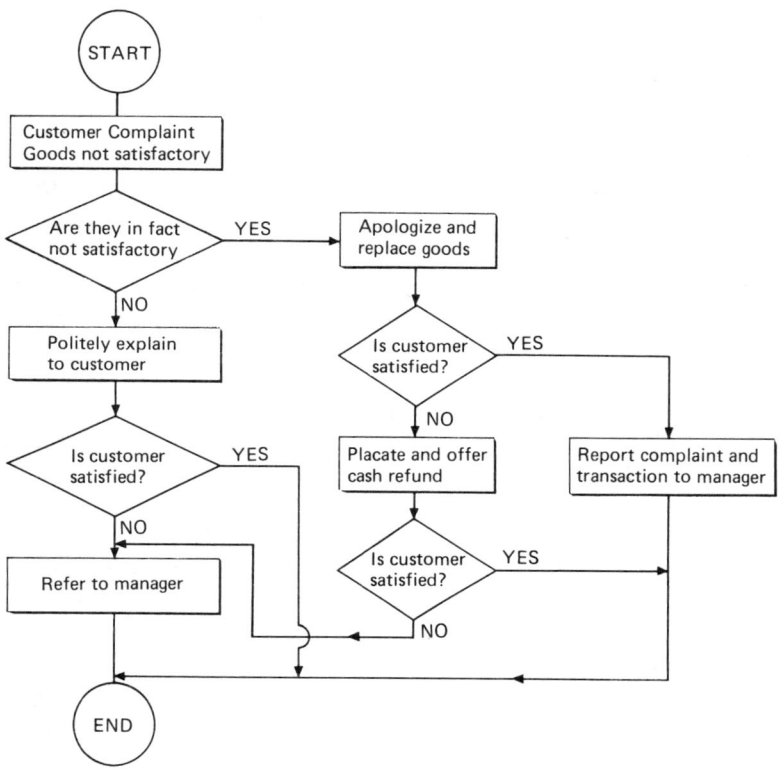

Fig. 16 *Algorithmic approach to sales training.*

frame. They have an extremely wide instructional application since any context involving choice or decision can be described as an algorithm. Widely used for fault-finding charts, identification keys and basic calculations, the use of an algorithm avoids the need for instruction altogether, or can be used as post-instructional training material. In this form they can be retained by trainees for permanent *aides-memoire* and reference, and as a testing implement. If the student can design one, they demonstrate a complete grasp of the subject. A very simple example of a short algorithm is shown in fig. 16. In fact a hierarchy of algorithms can be written for any subject and, taken to its logical conclusion, the basic algorithm may be condensed until it vanishes!

Do-it-Yourself Learning

Projects/Assignments

These are methods of discovery or 'experiential' learning which give the trainee great opportunity to display initiative and creativity. The task or end product is laid down by the trainer and resources may be listed for the trainee to research if desired, but the lines to be followed in reaching the objective are left completely to the trainee. Another highly active learning situation, it is ideal for the busy trainer, who has trainees with some intelligence and motivation, for whom knowledge acquisition is the expected learning outcome. From experience, it seems that the knowledge assignment is insufficiently exploited by trainers, who sometimes see learning situations purely in formal terms when, quite often, a trainee has the capacity and the desire to follow lines of his own in arriving at the training goal.

Again, importantly, it is a good method of assessing trainee's performance, providing feedback on a range of personal qualities, such as attitudes to the job and range of interests. It can be used in place of formal tests, but be wary of criticism of project work; trainees are not objective when experiential work is criticized, tending to take it as personal devaluation. Another important factor is in gaining the commitment of the trainee prior to project/assignment work. Since many hours may be spent in this activity it must therefore be seen to be directly relevant to the trainee's needs. Thus the briefing for this form of learning must be very carefully done, concentrating on mutual objectives and methods of achievement, planning co-operation and coaching where necessary. The trainer will need to prepare a formula for this type of learning and a suggested format is shown in fig. 17.

It will be seen from the example that there is a considerable saving in tutorial explanation of routines and in planning training sessions by didactic instructors. The preparation is restricted to filling in the objective and listing the basic resources; the trainee writing in his action plan and agreeing the completion date during the initial briefing interview.

Do-it-Yourself Learning

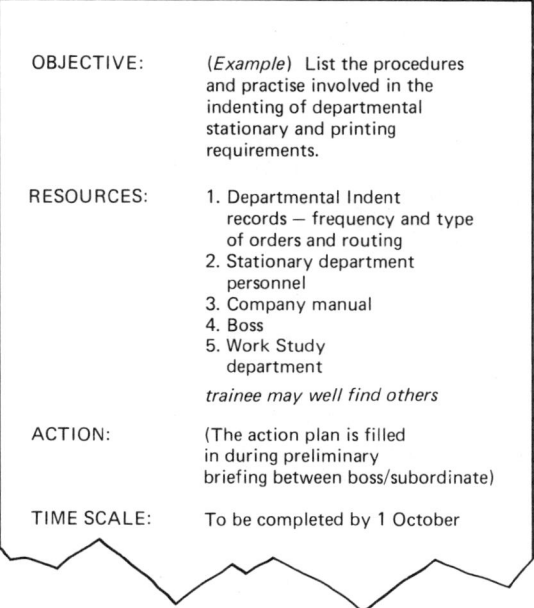

Fig. 17 Format for a learning assignment.

Group Dynamics

For the trainer who is skilled in interactive techniques, or has access to trained psychologists/sociologists in the work team, a valuable experiential learning situation exists in 'group dynamics'. This technique examines the behaviour of the individual in a group (and the group as a whole) and helps the trainee to learn the effects of his own behaviour upon others and his reactions to their behaviour towards him. By simply experiencing the situation, trainees become more enlightened about how and why people at work behave as they do, increase their communication skills and hopefully increase their self awareness and powers of observation.

A group task may be set, or the group allowed to decide its own way of structuring their time, and the *process* of what goes on is observed by the trained tutor. A plenary 'wash-up' session at the end allows discussion on how the group felt, and feedback to individual members is given by the tutor/observer. It is important that problems arising during the session are cleared up before the group breaks up. (The advantages of this technique for management and supervisory training are obvious and will be mentioned in the later chapter on this subject.) Points to watch are (a) that the observer records objectively, with some method of quantitative chart or score sheet, the intactions that occur (many systems of interactive analysis technique exist to aid this), (b) that concrete examples of behaviour patterns are illustrable and (c) that examinations of motives and private behaviour are used in a constructive rather than a destructive way and always at the discretion of the trainee. It is obvious that difficulties can arise if the trainee discovers something about himself that is distasteful to him, yet this may be necessary for his future growth. This is one reason why this method of training should be undertaken by trained people and the formation of the groups planned extremely carefully to give a correct mix. In the right hands however, it is a valuable means of self-discovery and bears further study in the 'training of attitudes towards people' in the working situation.

Laboratory Training

This is a development of the above and has a variety of names (sensitivity training, T-groups, D-groups, action-centred groups, etc.) but essentially similar procedures. Groups of trainees, usually of managerial or supervisory grade, spend a period of time together participating in group activities designed to promote understanding of themselves and each other. Personal problems and counselling may occur, role play or simulation exercises carried out and other interactive situations take place in a social vacuum, away from work with the participants stripped of rank. The success of the group depends upon the way that the members interact away from the organizational umbrella replacing dictated goals by their own. Essentially, by its very nature, laboratory training is outside the scope of the in-plant trainer, but for selected employees consul-

Do-it-Yourself Learning

tant trainers can be bought in (though the location would have to be different and the group mix preferably a vertical slice from differing disciplines). Usually however employees are sent away for specialist training on an external course.

These are just some of the techniques which involve the learner in an active role, the trainer becoming a planner of learning opportunities and a resource for help, advice and coaching (more of which in the chapter on management and supervisory development). Often trainers see their job as purely didactic teaching, with heavy emphasis on input. It is hoped that this superficial look at 'do-it-yourself' techniques will inspire the busy trainer to find out more about trainee-centred learning situations, with a view to increasing his own spare capacity as a manager – the key to adequate 'thinking time'.

Chapter Thirteen

Instructional Technique

The trainer has, by now decided upon his instructional objective, analysed the task, prepared a lesson plan, got everything ready and, we are assuming for this chapter, chosen a method of instruction involving input. A typical industrial training session might involve a short talk, followed by question, answer and testing on a knowledge item or a demonstration followed by supervised practice, on a skill item. The lesson plan will follow the commencement-core-conclusion format in each case and the trainer will have prepared his teaching area, laid out any materials or equipment necessary and, we hope, rehearsed the necessary skills, including the use of any visual aids he intends to use. Let us now examine some of the important factors in the actual delivery of his material.

Manner
The self-presentation of the trainer is very important. No-one learns when they are nervous, so it is desirable that the trainer's manner does not accentuate the natural fear of the unknown that new trainees always experience. Confidence (but not brashness) is the keynote, since at first they will rely heavily on his knowledge and must put their trust in him. A friendly approach is also necessary, with a sense of humour ideally, since it is important that the trainee feels that he is understood and cared about. A straightforward, adult interaction is the best learning situation, so it is important that 'superior' attitudes to trainees are avoided yet respect must be maintained, and some authorities would suggest, particularly with young trainees, that the emphasis should be on a nurturing parental role. However, certain cardinal sins must be ruled out, distracting mannerisms of all kinds, impatience, intolerance and inconsistency.

Appearance
Trainees will very likely have an expectation, however stereotyped, of the way an instructor in their particular industry should look. An important point, discussed in earlier chapters, is that of modelling; the way in which trainees copy the demeanour of their trainers. With these two factors in mind, the trainer will try to set an example in dress and general appearance, which will not differ too outlandishly from the accepted 'image' of his trade. Significant variations from the norm serve only to act as distractions in the learning situation and are not helpful to trainees.

Voice
One of the most potent influences in the training situation is the instructor's use of the voice. *Volume* is paramount, suited to the local acoustics and entirely audible at all times. *Pitch* must be considered, particularly in talks, since the rise and fall of inflexion obviates monotony. *Pace* is important, since too quick a speaking rate will fail to be understood and too slow a delivery will induce boredom and reduce momentum. *Emphasis*, particularly on key points (such as safety, hygiene, etc.), underlines the importance of the item. Avoid too many emphasized points or the effect will be lost, yet key factors must be punched home. *Pauses* punctuate the instruction, allow the trainee a mental breather and give the trainer time to glance at his lesson plan.

Eye contact
This is a problem to some trainers, particularly in group situations where trainees are listening to a knowledge input session. With experience, the trainer will avoid 'fixing' individual trainees (particularly if they are female!) since this causes embarrassment. The best compromise seems to be, in Army terms, to look at their 'cap badge', i.e. eyes travelling gently around the group whilst teaching, at just above eye level. (Avoid too quick a movement or it will seem like a Wimbledon spectator!) If the trainees are arranged in a horseshoe or three sides of a square formation, problems will be found on both 'wings', i.e. the trainer will tend to ignore the extreme right and

Instructional Technique

left hand sides of the group. Remember to include these people and, as a precaution, place trainees who are likely to be strong contributors to question and answer sessions in these positions. During question and answer, it is perfectly correct to make definite eye contact whilst the trainee is asking a question, or when eliciting responses from individual trainees. (It is usual for people to look at others when seeking information and to free their gaze when giving it, according to behavioural scientists.)

Questioning
This topic deserves a book to itself, since it forms the fulcrum of the participative style of teaching and is the basis for good rapport between trainer and trainee. There are a number of reasons for asking questions during a training session:

> To encourage participation, thereby increasing interest and activity.
> To give feedback to the trainer that he is progressing at a rate the trainees can cope with.
> To encourage reasoning ability in the trainees.
> To test trainees' knowledge.
> To maintain control of errant trainees.

It will be seen from this list that the first three types of question differ in character from the last two, since the latter are to do with testing, whereas the former encourage thought and help the session to develop. Terms have been coined to differentiate the two as testing questions and teaching questions and although this is a great over-simplification in some ways, it is sufficient for the industrial trainer. *Testing questions* essentially check that learning has, in fact, taken place and are historical in nature since they test previous knowledge. *Teaching questions* form the framework of the session, asking the trainee to reason out principles, to describe concepts and to forecast the next step, so in essence they are based in the present and the future. For example, a teaching question might be: 'What do you think makes this part of the machine go up and down,

Instructional Technique

Fred?' or 'How, do you imagine, can we allow for depreciation of machinery in our cost analysis?'. On these same points a testing question might be 'Can you remember what makes this part of the machine go up and down, Fred?' or 'Where did we put depreciation of machinery in our cost analysis?'. Teaching questions are the hardest to frame, but with care and prior thought, they can form the core of the session, particularly if used in conjunction with visual presentation of the answers on a board, as outlined in earlier chapters.

Framing questions in general is an art which requires constant practice. There are some ground rules however:

Use language trainees will understand.
Start with a question word (who, why, where, what, when, how?)
Use testing questions to check previous knowledge at commencement and conclusion and teaching questions during the core.
Try to ask questions (for maximum participation) at the rate of one every one to two minutes.
In group situations the rule is Pose, Pause, Pounce! In other words, put the question to the group as a whole, pause, and if nothing happens, ask one trainee for his answer. The 'pause' is essential for thinking time, and trainers must learn to withstand the pressure of silence. Trainers new to this will find it a lengthy business, but at all costs avoid the temptation to leap in. Eventually this will become second nature, but at first some device such as counting, or reciting the question silently to oneself, are a useful barrier to rushing in.

Usually someone will answer after the pause for thought, and the way the trainer deals with this answer is critical, since it sets the tone for the session and can kill or encourage other trainees' participation. If the answer is correct, reinforce the student's action by immediate acknowledgement ('Good', 'Fine', 'Yes'), by perhaps rephrasing it and using it in the development of the next teaching point. If the answer is not what was required, but the trainer feels the question was reasonable, it is good practice to ask for someone else's view, not to say 'No!', as this will perhaps affect that trainee's future input. If no-one comes in,

Instructional Technique

there is a fair chance that the question was not framed clearly, and good policy is to rephrase it and ask the original trainee, thus saving his face. Avoid questions which have a yes/no answer, since the trainees have a fifty-fifty chance of guessing correctly, and if a yes/no answer does emerge, it should be followed by 'Why?' to the same trainee.

At the beginning of this section, one purpose of questioning was stated to be the control of errant trainees. Trainees who are not concentrating can be brought gently to heel by naming them first, i.e. pounce, pause, pose! The sharp emphasis on their name usually causes a momentary start of surprise which is sufficient to engage their grey matter to the point in question and their reply to the testing question indicates whether they have assimilated the required facts.

In general, be gentle in question and answer sessions, treat contributions with respect and encourage verbalization of points which are not clear. If the trainees are afraid, they will not ask for clarification when needed, and will not 'spark' spontaneously when creative leaps are made. Question technique is a difficult art to master, but the reward of a lively, interactive group learning together is one of the trainer's most valuable experiences.

Use of display summaries
Without wishing to duplicate material already discussed in the chapter on visual aids, it may be worthwhile to give a further reminder that the lesson plan should show when to employ a display summary and when to remove it to prevent distraction. When using flipcharts and boards in an extemporized fashion as the lesson goes on, some reminders are useful:

> Always write up the title of the session.
>
> Write large enough to be seen by all.
>
> Acknowledge correct answers to questions by writing up on display summary.
>
> Do not doodle on displays to be copied down by trainees. (Sketch on separate displays.)
>
> With flipcharts, words which are difficult to spell can be lightly pencilled in previously – the trainees will not be

Instructional Technique

able to see it! Similarly with totals, calculations and answers, these can be pencilled in to save time.

Use of colour to highlight different parts of the display is recommended.

Beware of turning one's back when writing on boards; a style in which the trainer stands alongside the board, writing across it, is easily cultivated.

Make sure the display summary is visible to all (remember the 'wingers'!).

Always display new words, people's names and foreign references, even if only using headings.

Do not be in too much of a hurry to destroy extemporized display summaries – quite often trainees will need to refer to them later.

The display summary is an important part of a knowledge-type session, since not only does it reinforce the key points as they are made, but also forms the basis for trainees' notes. Properly used, it helps to add pause and emphasis to a session, allowing time for the trainees to think and giving the trainer time to check his lesson plan. It also adds variety to the lesson and gives trainees a break from the instructor's voice!

Trainee's notes

These are an integral part of any theory session and some care should be taken by the trainer in deciding which method the trainees will be recommended to adopt. Much depends on the purpose that such notes will serve, whether it is for future reference, as the basis for some action or to supplement the teaching session. Basically trainees' notes fall into two categories; those made or prepared by the trainees themselves and those pre-prepared by the trainer, as in the form of a handout.

Of the types made by the trainees themselves, *dictation* always seems to be the least effective with its inbuilt spelling errors and use of one sense only, the trainees listening but not necessarily understanding. Taking notes *on their own initiative* is acceptable only where the trainees are of a high educational standard, since this method requires long practice if a successful record of

Instructional Technique

the session is to be achieved. *Copying display summaries* is much more satisfactory since the trainer has more control over the material entering the students' notebooks, though it does involve the trainer in laborious board work.

Of the types *pre-prepared* by the trainer, several formats can be used:

> Summary or headings – used mainly as an *aide-memoire* of the key points. Brevity and relevance are essential with bold headings and generous spacing.
>
> Partially completed handouts – in this format sufficient space is left for the trainee to write in some notes within the set framework (more active, with some choice as to quantity of material necessary for each individual).
>
> Examples and outlines – often used in quantitative teaching where worked examples or models are presented – together with room for the trainee's own work. Used effectively in costing, accountancy, scientific and other allied training.
>
> Check lists and procedures – often following a skill-type session to remind trainees of a series of activities which have to be carried out in sequence. Ideal as memory joggers back on the job, they can often be a lifeline to the confused new employee.
>
> Books and pamphlets provide background about a subject or easily digestible guides to more complex material (e.g. 'A Guide to Health and Safety at Work Act 1974' is a useful follow up to a talk on this subject). Such material is often provided free of charge from interested bodies such as government agencies etc.

Some problems are associated with pre-prepared material, however. The first and most obvious is cost in labour and materials. It also tends to be taken for granted and not valued as much as notes taken personally. There is no guarantee that complex pre-prepared material is understood, especially background reading, and indeed there is no guarantee that they are ever read. Finally note-taking is still a skill which will stand a trainee in good stead whatever his future role, and as such could be put forward as an argument for active note-taking. However, with these provisos, the handout is a very useful contribution to effective training and, where accurate recall of information is essential, is well worth the time and cost to the trainer in prior preparation.

Sequence
During our earlier look at the learning process, we perceived that, although sequential, logical progression of instruction was generally desirable, in some skill-type instructions learning was made easier if critical psychomotor activities were taught and practised separately. We instanced the separation of sewing machinists' training of guiding, machine control, threading up etc., all taught separately and subsequently combined, and one could parallel this in car driving with use of controls, clutch operation, steering etc. by systematic analysis of the skills involved. By and large however, the stage-by-stage process of instruction follows a pre-determined sequence from known to unknown, simple to complex and when discussing instructional technique, sufficient stress cannot be placed on the need to teach in a logical progression. The learning process requires organization, ease of memorization and recall to be successful, and so the trainer needs to be ordered in his presentation of material. To this end, various checklists (including the famous TWI Job Instruction) have been produced over the years as guides to trainers; and the author is often asked for step-by-step guides to instructing. At the risk, then, of being simplistic, since the individual trainer will inevitably modify anyone else's concept, it might be useful to produce *aides-memoire* for just three methods of instruction – the skill type (demonstration), knowledge type (talk) and attitude type (discussion) – in most common use and hope that trainers will develop their own 'crib-sheets' for other methods of instruction they adopt. Also one could perhaps make a plea that trainers take a leaf out of the systematic skill analyst's book and practise separately those techniques most necessary for overall satisfactory teaching, e.g. use of visuals, question technique, voice production etc., finally combining them into a complete lesson, using all the skills practised.

Instructional Technique

SKILL TYPE INSTRUCTION

EXAMPLE: DEMONSTRATION & PRACTICE METHOD

---

1. **PREPARATION**

    Check: Amount & type of trainees.
    Previous knowledge.
    Prepare: Instructional objective.
    Lesson plan (from analyses).
    Materials.
    Equipment and Tools.
    Visual Aids.
    Workplace Layout.
    Rehearse: Task
    To target time.
    To quality standard.
    Timing of whole demonstration.

2. **PREPARE TRAINEE FOR INSTRUCTION**

    Introductions.
    Induction (if done by trainer).

    COMMENCEMENT
    - Put at ease.
    - Create interest in task.
    - Check previous knowledge.
    - Ensure correct position.

3. **PRESENTATION**

    CORE
    - Get attention.
    - Demonstrate task at correct speed silently.
    - Demonstrate stage by stage with question and answer.
    - Demonstrate task to target with commentary.
    - Check using testing questions.

4. PRACTICE

CONCLUSION
- Allow one trainee to try task and discuss performance.
- Tell trainees exactly what is expected.
- Disperse to practise.

5. SUPERVISION AND COACHING

COACH
- Supervise until correct.
- Act as coach as errors occur.
- Check trainees' work.
- Give feedback immediately.
- Mark work if control system is in operation.
- Assess overall performance for reporting.

6. PUT TO WORK

- Indicate personal responsibilities.
- Link to future.
- Name person who will help.
- Aid transfer problems by being available.
- Check as necessary for follow-up reporting.

Instructional Technique

KNOWLEDGE TYPE INSTRUCTION

EXAMPLE: TALK/LESSON METHOD

1. PREPARATION	Check: Training programme for amount and type of trainees. Prepare: Instructional objective. Lesson plan. Visual material. Equipment. Trainees' notes (if prepared, e.g. handouts). Rehearse: Timing and presentation. Use of visual aids.
2. COMMENCEMENT	Introductions (if necessary). Put at ease. Focus interest — ? topical. / ? historical. / ? humourous. / ? impact. Need to know. How far today (range). Title.
3. CORE	Lead off with general teaching question. Develop material step by step. Maintain interest by — voice. / manner. / emphasis. / variety. / visual. / material. / eye contact.

Instructional Technique

	Use display summary at each stage (either pre-prepared or extemporized). Encourage participation with question technique (at least one per minute). Stress key points (must know). Supervise trainees' notes.
4. CONCLUSION	Go over key points again. Give trainee opportunity to ask questions. Test assimilation by objective testing. Link to future. Follow up to evaluate success.

Instructional Technique

ATTITUDE TYPE INSTRUCTION

EXAMPLE: DISCUSSION GROUP (ASSOCIATIVE TYPE)

1. PREPARATION

    Lesson plan including:
    Title.
    The position to date – commencement.
    Sequence of questions for core.
    Visual material if necessary.
    Pre-printed discussion material.
    Research personal background of group members.

2. COMMENCEMENT

    Introduce all members to each other and yourself (chairman).
    Put at ease.
    Introduce topic, giving background and position to date (keep it short).
    Lead off with general question.

3. CORE

    Act as referee objectively.
    Seek views of all members – encourage the shy, control the over-talkative.
    Beware of: side-tracking.
       settling old scores.
       vague remarks.
    Make notes of important points.
    Summarize the position from time to time, objectively.

Instructional Technique

Use expertise within group, personally known to you.
If discussion flags: throw in new question,
ask individuals for their experience,
encourage reticent.

4. CONCLUSION

Summarize position.
Clarify any doubts about individual views.
Reconcile opinions if necessary.
Assess the result objectively.
Indicate own view, but stress importance of group decision.
Thank participants.
Link to future use.

5. FOLLOW UP

Make use of discussion by submitting report (with minutes if necessary).
Take action where possible (to ensure credibility).
Check changes in attitude of group members.

Chapter Fourteen

Monitoring Trainees' Performance and Analysing Faults

The importance of rapid feedback to the trainer so that he has knowledge of results has already been emphasized. Quick and accurate monitoring and assessment provide great incentives to learning progress, so it is essential that the trainer does not feel that his work is done when the presentation is over. It is traditionally supposed that the measurement of performance is left in the hands of the instructor, but many good training schemes allow the trainee to monitor his own performance wherever practicable, since he learns best by recognizing his own errors and being able to correct them. This means that an efficient control and marking system must be designed as a tool for the trainee; the work that this entails however is amply repaid in the reduction in delay between error and correction. This also helps to develop the trainee's responsibility for his own learning and the trust and recognition gained from acknowledging the trainee's maturity is a great incentive in the learning process.

However, whether instructor or learner-centred, measurement of performance is essential for checking the achievement of instructional objectives. In monitoring performance, the advantages of setting accurate behavioural objectives at the beginning will be demonstrated by the ease in which the changes in behaviour can be measured. The standards of performance most often used are time and quality in skill-type instruction, and time and accuracy of recall in knowledge training. The determination of targets is a key factor; to aid this one must go back, as always, to learning theory. It will be remembered that training periods are best limited to forty-five minutes maximum on one exercise. After this time concentration wavers and variety of activity is needed to raise the learner's

Monitoring Trainees' Performance and Analysing Faults

motivational level. So here is a natural limit to activity, and within this period the trainee should preferably have completed a new step in his programme. Within this constraint, the trainee may have several graded attempts at the task and he should see noticeable improvement in his attainment by the end. It is by the achievement of carefully set targets, within his reach but not too easy, that confidence is built up, as we have seen in earlier chapters. It is important to set one's target times carefully, with the trainee in mind, remembering that it is

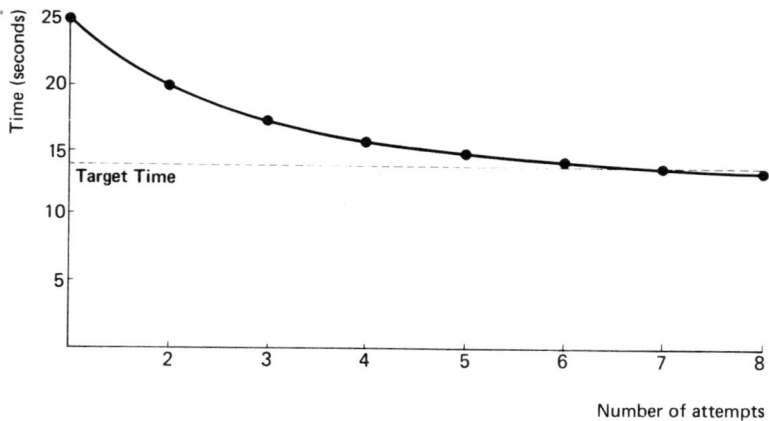

Fig. 18 Time graph suitable for short periods of training.

better to present an activity in a series of stages, with graded targets for each stage, than to repeat an activity with a high target over a number of sessions.

Targets for training exercises, as stated earlier, may be of different kinds. In skills training, where speed of execution is paramount, a *timed* target is most common and can be expressed in two ways. A list of the number of attempts compared with the time taken for each attempt is the simplest way. Alternatively the information can be expressed graphically with time taken on the vertical axis and number of attempts on the horizontal as in fig. 18.

Monitoring Trainees' Performance and Analysing Faults

There is a school of thought, however, that favours a graph which climbs upwards in decreasing gains since this, they argue, increases motivation. Certainly for tasks requiring longer periods of practice, this may be so, but it will be seen that to present the material in this way the scores have to be expressed as performance ratings. It is common these days for experienced worker standard (EWS) to be rated as 100 performance (this conforms with work study and standard costing criteria), but sometimes piece work (incentive) performance, rated at 133, is used. Whichever method of rating is employed, and it is not the purpose of this book to enter an old argument, the performance rating is sited on the vertical axis and the time span along the horizontal axis as seen in fig. 19.

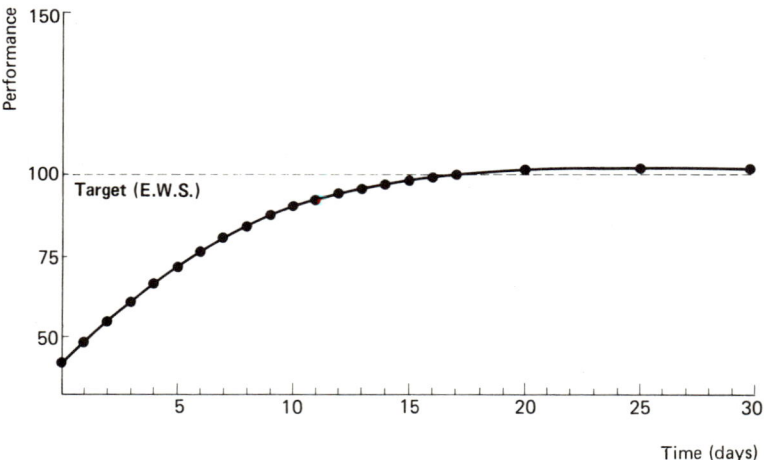

Fig. 19 Learning curve suitable for longer training periods.

Time is not the only measure of performance, quality can be measured by the number of faults made during a practice session. (This can also be applied to knowledge assimilation expressed as the number of mistakes.) This will result in a downward graph, as in fig. 20.

Monitoring Trainees' Performance and Analysing Faults

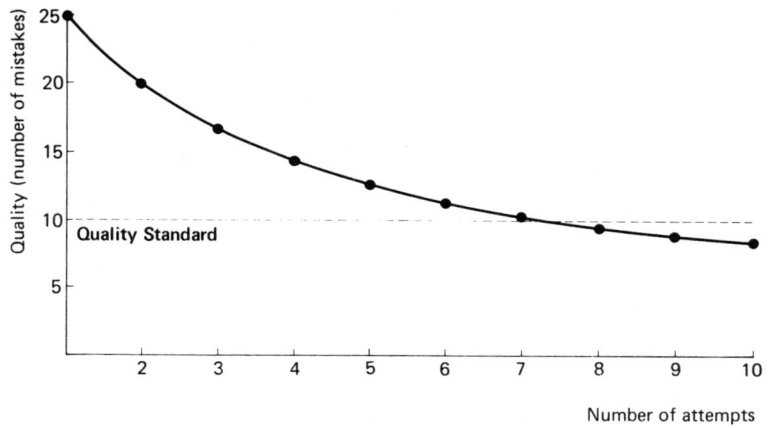

Fig. 20   Quality graph showing number of mistakes.

Again there is a motivational advantage in seeing an upward curve as quality increases. To achieve this, some quantitative assessment of the seriousness of the error expressed as a percentage figure is necessary, i.e. if ninety centimetres of stitching were correct out of one hundred centimetres or ninety words from a list of one hundred correctly memorized then this could be expressed as 90% – this figure being used on the vertical axis. The result is shown in fig. 21.

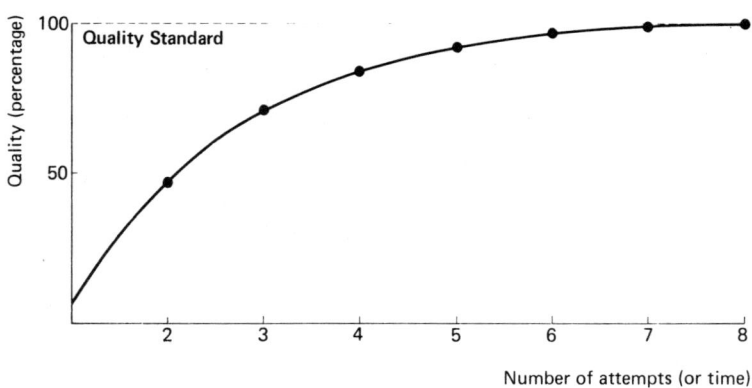

Fig. 21   Quality graph expressed in percentages.

It is possible of course to show both speed and quality performance on the same graph using the above method, by the use of separate colours. Bar charts can also be used to illustrate increased performance dramatically, and trainees can be taught to draw their own graphs and bar charts from their recordings of speed and quality. Apart from the excellent feedback this gives, it is often a welcome break from practice sessions, giving the trainer time to counsel appropriately and individually. Whilst the use of such monitoring devices is common in skill teaching, not enough use is made of visual presentation of scores (rather than by lists of figures) in knowledge type instruction, where percentage scores in tests provide good performance data, if properly graded, as in fig. 22. (Some considerable motivation can be generated by trainees competing against one another to reach targets when graphically presented.)

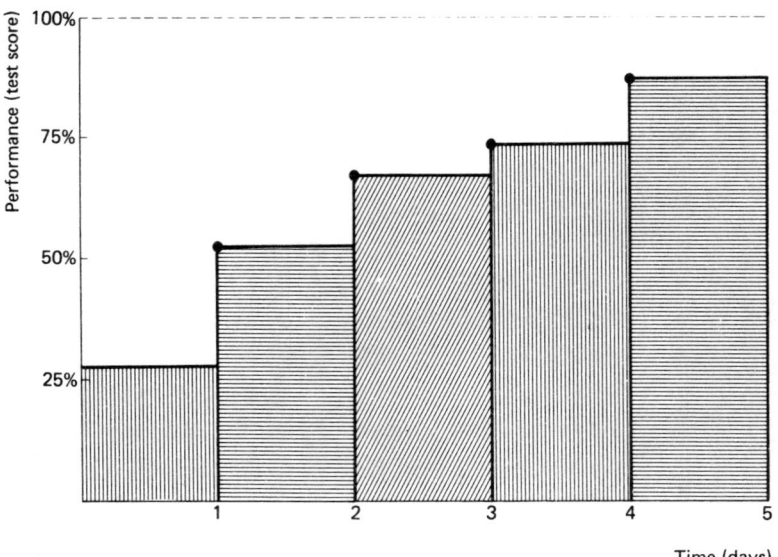

Fig. 22 Bar chart presentation of knowledge pickup.

Monitoring Trainees' Performance and Analysing Faults

Other performance recording systems use the estimated earnings of the trainee as a standard, using a nomograph or other device which relates speed performance to the piece work rate or standard costings. This has a definite motivational effect upon the trainee as he sees his target times in relation to his potential piece-rate earnings (without waiting time), and can monitor his own performance towards experienced worker standard, i.e. when he leaves the training school. Slightly more complicated to set up, this system must use the factory method of incentive payment and recording system along the vertical axis, with duration of training along the horizontal axis, as in fig. 23.

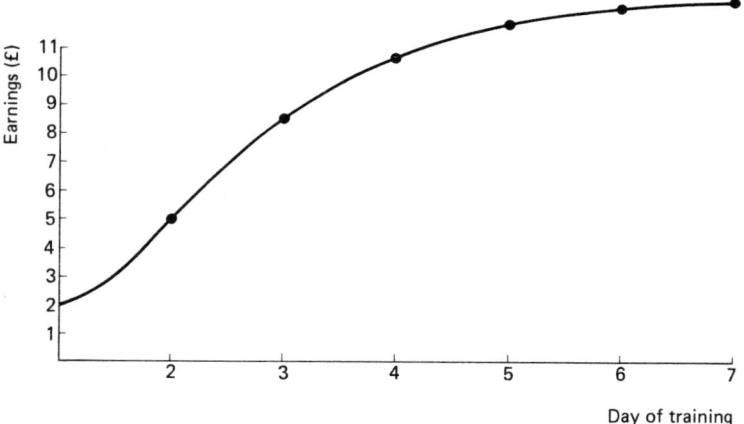

Fig. 23   Graph showing trainee's estimated earnings.

Apart from the recording of trainees' progress as an individual chart or work sheet, the trainer has to keep a certain amount of paperwork up to date if he has more than one trainee to deal with, and his monitoring system should include the following.

115

Monitoring Trainees' Performance and Analysing Faults

Progress chart
This should cover all trainees under his control, with names along the left and exercises or tasks instructed and practised (usually filled in when the trainee is proficient) across the page. A more elaborate code can be used to show what stage the trainee is at, i.e. whether demonstrated to, practising under supervision or achieving EWS. This is especially useful, where

Name of trainee	USE OF KITCHEN EQUIPMENT	KNIFE DRILL	PREPARATION OF VEGETABLES	PREPARATION AND COOKING SAUCES	NUTRITION	PORTION CONTROL	DISHING AND SERVING
A. Middleton	●◐○	●◐○	●◐				
D. Jones	●◐○	●◐					
C. Hopkins	●◐○	●◐○	●◐○	●◐			
D. Thomas	●◐○	●◐○	●◐○	●◐○	●◐	●	
R. Stevens	●◐○	●◐○	●◐	●			
LEGEND	● Demonstrated		◐ Improving		○ Proficient		

Fig. 24 *Trainee's progress chart (example: commis school meals cook).*

(as in a busy ward in a hospital with a sister using training opportunities to demonstrate certain procedures to individual students) the trainees will be taught as and when the on-job tutor has time. There are pros and cons as to whether the trainer displays his progress chart in the office where all can see, thus introducing a competitive element, or whether he keeps a private record so as not to panic the apprehensive trainee (who may compare how much he has achieved with what he should have done by this time!). A typical progress chart is shown in fig. 24.

Daily programme
In large training schemes a daily programme will be needed to show exactly what exercises or tasks the trainees will be working on. Needless to say, this has to be worked out the day prior to the operation of the programme, and leads to the issuing of a *daily work sheet* for each trainee, showing details of the items to be attempted.

Weekly/monthly report
Other documents which arise from training schemes are the weekly/monthly report form which is a summary of the work carried out by trainees during the period stated. This will be necessary for completing trainees' records, liaison with outside bodies such as ITBs, City and Guilds joint schemes etc. An assessment of each individual is usually called for at these periods, to enable management to review the trainee's progress and control the training budget.

Faults Analysis

A properly trained employee should be able to recognize any faults that may arise during the performance of his tasks, and respond quickly to them. This ability to handle faults may in some cases be the most important part of a job, especially in many routine manual tasks, where it may be the only 'skilled' aspect of the whole operation. To enable trainees to monitor their own quality performance, the trainer in many cases must embark on a *faults analysis* and present them with the fruits of this, a *fault diagnosis*, since this is the essential piece of information the trainee needs in order to remedy his errors.

The most common method of analysing faults uses seven columns (each heading can be remembered by the mnemonic FACERAP) as in the example shown in fig. 25.

Fault This is the common name of the fault, by which it is known in the individual establishment.

Appearance How is the fault recognized? What do we look for?

Cause What are the possible causes of the fault? Is it mechanical, material, previous operations, or human error?

Monitoring Trainees' Performance and Analysing Faults

Fault Analysis Worksheet

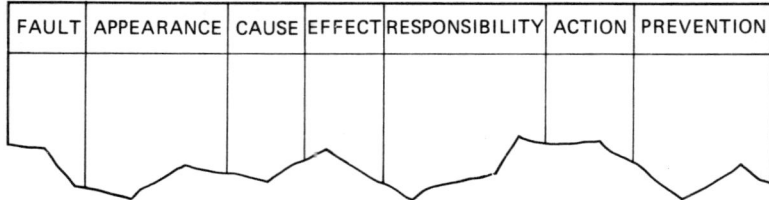

Fig. 25 Layout of fault analysis worksheet.

Effect What effects does the fault have? Who is affected? Does it spoil the product or severely hamper the next operation?
Responsibility Whose responsibility is the fault?
Action What immediate action must be taken?
Prevention How can we stop the fault from recurring?

In practice, it is sometimes difficult to decide in which column certain entries should be made. This is particularly so in the case of 'responsibility', since it could be a combination of people, and in 'appearance' and 'effect' which are sometimes identical. The whole process revolves around the premise that

FAULT: LUMPY GRAVY					
APPEARANCE	CAUSE	EFFECT	RESPONSIBILITY	ACTION	PREVENTION
Lumps can be seen in gravy when stirred	1. Thickening agent stirred into hot water direct 2. Thickening not dissolved properly in cold water 3. Gravy not stirred whilst coming to boil 4. Heat too high	Customer complaint Loss of customer Loss of profit	Sauce cook	Useless Dispose of	1+2. Dissolve thickening correctly. 3. Stir gravy whilst bringing to boil 4. Control heat more accurately.

Fig. 26 Fault analysis worksheet with an example.

Monitoring Trainees' Performance and Analysing Faults

prevention is better than cure, and the efficient instructor will aim to include the results of column seven (prevention) in his initial instruction, giving the reasons for certain precautions from a sound analytical base. The example in fig. 26 shows how the FACERAP chart is filled in, using a simple illustration.

Faults analysis, like job analysis, can however lead to a mass of material, some of which is not relevant to the trainee. All the trainee needs in practice is the symptoms of faults, the warning signals, and how to avoid them, or put them right. So the usual presentation of fault training to the student is in the form of a *faults diagnosis* sheet, containing only information that he is directly interested in. This teaching format can be presented in many ways, but a very convenient method is to produce cards drawn up as in fig. 27.

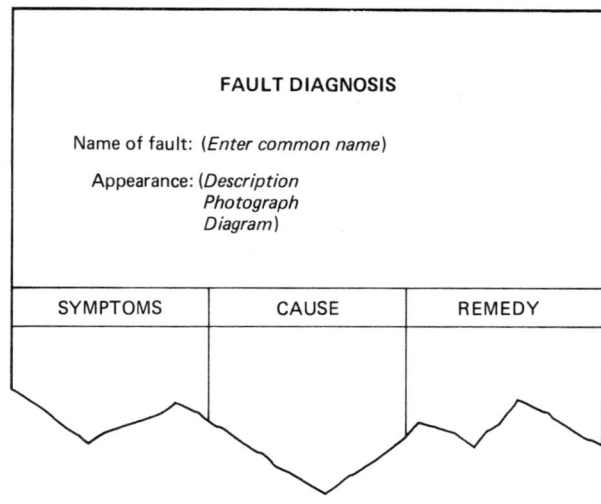

Fig. 27   Fault diagnosis card.

Fault analysis and diagnosis have a direct bearing on the training process, since the trainee will be more able to monitor his own quality performance and will have had prior instruction on what to do if faults occur. This builds confidence in the

Monitoring Trainees' Performance and Analysing Faults

instructor's foresight, aids the trainee's powers of observation and can prevent much wastage of materials and rework costs, since the trainer may not be in a position to supervise and correct errors all the time. Meticulous attention to detail may be necessary during the analysis stage, but this will be amply repaid when trainees are able to spot faults immediately they occur.

Chapter Fifteen

The Training of Supervisors and Managers

All commercial enterprises depend upon a continuous supply of supervisors and managers at all levels to meet the future needs of the business. It is fashionable to term the training of these people *management development* and indeed this term has some validity in that a secondary objective is to improve the job performance of existing managers and to help to prepare them for promotion. It also includes the instruction of potential managers who may rise from the 'shop floor' to be groomed as charge hands, foremen and superintendents, since supervision is, without doubt, the first line of management.

Managers learn mostly by managing, it has been said, i.e. there is no substitute for experience gained on the job, and to a great extent this is true, yet there are genuine advantages in using external specialists, off-job training in specialized institutions and interaction with managers from other industries on courses etc. The best management training will probably combine all of these elements, looking at the training and development needs of individual managers.

The first essential in any management development scheme is a policy setting out objectives, in terms which are clearly understood at all levels of the company. It is important that not only is this policy agreed at the highest level (the board of directors, or its equivalent) but is also publicized throughout the hierarchies of the firm. Top management must be directly involved in this policy making, since organizational planning must include personnel (and therefore training) strategies at the same stage of decision making as new products, technology, investment or markets. Overall planning is needed to forecast future needs and to design the succession plans which will provide the managerial staff to meet these future commitments.

This is where training as an act of faith ends and planning to meet future management manpower needs begins.

How do we know who are the likely targets for such training policies? The answer must surely be in an efficient appraisal procedure. If the development plan is not only to meet organizational needs, but to aid individuals to meet their personal career goals, someone has to know what each man wants, understand his needs and do something about it. This man is usually 'the boss', i.e. one's immediate superior, who is probably the most powerful influence in a manager's development, whatever the organization. Inescapably then, management development is thus the responsibility of line managers, who need to be trained in performance appraisals (including interviewing procedure) and how to use the information gained in a variety of ways, such as promotion, job rotation, planned experience etc. An appraisal scheme should identify the training needs of the individual, i.e. the gap between the knowledge, skills and attitudes that the job demands and those already possessed. It should also set about procedures which will fill these gaps in a systematic way by planned development, with effective review sessions between boss/subordinates at regular intervals.

One way in which this planned development can take place on the job is by coaching. To quote the Department of Employment's *Glossary of Training Terms*, coaching is the process of 'systematically increasing the ability and experience of the trainee by giving him planned tasks coupled with continuous appraisal and counselling by the trainee's supervisor'. Opportunities occur in everyday working relationships to develop skills, to train the subordinate, at times other than when the formal staff appraisal is carried out. Unfortunately, line managers are not adept at recognizing 'the trainable moment' and seizing upon it to help develop their subordinates. It is not an easy matter to pursue maximum efficiency and still develop subordinates – it calls for skill and effort on the part of the boss. The coaching skills necessary are not naturally widely distributed among line managers and must be actively encouraged to flourish, i.e. it should be an explicit requirement in job descriptions and 'natural' coaches should be rewarded and recognized. There are certain advantages in the coaching role – the coach who is successful can delegate with a light heart and managers whose protégées make good can expect further trainees to help them.

What does the successful coach do? He (a) sets tasks and assignments, (b) monitors progress and assesses performance and (c) gives adequate feedback and discussion.

In the first duty, he must be systematic about the sort of assignments that he sets. An arrangement, almost like MBO (Management by Objectives), allowing a measure of participation in setting targets, is essential, with a completion deadline set to the ability and experience of the trainee. These assignments can be made progressively more challenging, with review meetings at regular intervals to discuss progress, analyse reports and map out future development. The line manager must be careful to give impartial, objective feedback and not respond directly to cries for help. He must develop question technique to throw the ball back into the trainee's court, with queries such as 'How are you going to go about such and such?' or 'What do you suggest is the best method for obtaining this information?'

In reviewing performance, an informal technique of 'How did it go?', 'How did you get on with so-and-so?', 'How could we do even better?' questioning style seems to work well. Formal appraisal will naturally arise out of such sessions, but not as an unwelcome, once-and-for-all intrusion by an almost perfect stranger of a boss – so often the cry of the appraised in many industries. Another important facet is openness. The boss who shares information discreetly, who shows his subordinates the reports and memoranda which directly affect the task and who sometimes shares his own problems, may well be surprised at the degree of help and support that can accrue 'out of the mouths of babes and sucklings'.

So far we have only discussed the development of managers on-the-job, but there are two further possibilities. The first is the establishment of a recognized management centre for training, a sort of staff college, in which the supervisory and managerial instruction for the organization is carried out off the job. There are considerable advantages to such an establishment;

the board is seen to be 'putting its money where its mouth is', i.e. there is a concrete commitment to development, a symbol of the organization's will to carry out its policies. Secondly, such places become a forum for management and supervisory communication providing valuable feedback to the company on morale and opinion throughout the firm. Lastly, since the company controls the input policy, training can be tailor-made to its requirements, can modify course and content and method effectively and it comes as no surprise to find that those organizations with their own training establishments tend to put high effort into their development programmes. (Since the Industrial Training Act, certain funds have been available through the ITBs for firms wishing to set up such training centres – an additional incentive.)

Lastly, there are the benefits obtained from using completely external resources, e.g. consultant trainers, college courses etc. Whilst appearing to be rather 'old hat', the full and part-time courses at local colleges are still a valuable learning method and a means of exchanging experience, on an interdisciplinary and inter-firm basis. The Diploma in Management Studies, the professional examinations in Works Management, Cost Accounting, Marketing, Personnel and Administrative Management are still the main stream method of gaining acceptable qualifications for managers and the National Examinations Board in Supervisory Studies (NEBSS). Certificate and Diploma still provides off-job supervisory training to a high standard on the theory side, and to a certain extent (with in-built project work) on practical skills. The release of staff for such courses can be a considerable bonus to recruitment and word-of-mouth recommendation where job applications are concerned and the act of sending people to college in the company's time is another way of demonstrating the support of top management in training policies.

'Buying-in' management training consultants can be an expensive business. However, the advantages of a fresh, uncluttered approach to management training can result in considerable cost savings as against internal 'trainers' of dubious expertise. The professionalism of consultants varies, but experimentation with their use can not only provide training courses, but the way in which the consultants approach their task is a valuable learning experience and they can be used in a developmental role for internal training staff.

Analysing Management Training Needs

As with all other branches of training, the first question to be asked is 'What do managers need to know?'. When analysing the training needs of managers, the usual questions follow on, 'How much do they know already?' and 'At what level of the hierarchy will they operate?'.

If the manager is to operate at first-line supervisory level he will need to have a vastly different syllabus from the director. In general, supervisors will need knowledge, skills and attitudes directly related to leadership and technical expertise. An analysis of his job will show that he must effectively:

Motivate.	Solve problems of a technical nature.
Communicate.	Carry out policies.
Direct.	Discipline.
Train.	Reward.

Such people are the link between the workforce and management, and need to have the 'common touch' to enable them to know empathetically the problems and rewards of shop-floor life. Yet they must have an appreciation of policy, the day-to-day politics of the organization and a real flair for human relations. The trainer at this level must be able to speak the language of the eminently practical world of doing things, so any courses or development aimed at this level must be couched in down-to-earth, pragmatic common sense, with plenty of concrete examples to support concepts.

Training and development for top managers will stress topics such as finance, formation of policy delegation, organizational theory, industrial relations, political and governmental bodies, the company abroad, public relations, industrial law, and economics. By and large, top managers need have little technical expertise within the company's specialisms, their knowledge and skills being based on the ability to control their company's relationships with the outside world. They need to know exactly the firm's standing within the economic, political and social environment and will need to think creatively with a high degree of conceptual skill. The top executive must be able to:

Forecast.	Lead.
Plan.	Delegate.
Formulate policy.	Influence and persuade.
Deal with outside bodies.	Speak in public.
	Be 'good at meetings'.
Integrate varying disciplines.	Appreciate technical processes and limitations.

Middle managers have jobs which contain elements of both areas of training need, but since they execute policy will need more in the way of 'how to' technical information, both about the product and the means of achieving targets. In addition to certain of the top manager's attributes, he will need a thorough knowledge of:

Production planning.	Industrial relations.
Cost analysis.	Management services (work study, CPA etc.).
Personnel administration.	
Data processing.	Operations Research.

He will of course in addition need the human relations, leadership and delegation skills that all managers require, but the emphasis is on more conceptual training than is the case at first-line level.

As has been stated earlier the most opportune time for individual analysis of training needs occurs during the appraisal procedure. During this process, the individual manager can be assessed as to his future needs and particularly the preferred learning style of that person. Some managers learn best by on-job training and some by formal courses. The appraisal process will probably lead to a balance of the two using courses for specific knowledge requirements and job experience such as coaching, understudying and job rotation to achieve the required practical applications.

The Training of Supervisors and Managers

In conclusion, let us take a look at the typical subject matter for a management training course and some of the appropriate strategies for teaching each topic:

COMPANY KNOWLEDGE

1. Objectives, philosophy and history
2. Policies and procedures
3. Products and services
4. Organization structure
5. Economic policies and finance
6. Geography – plants and factories
7. Industrial relations policy
8. Social and Welfare facilities

Lectures, talks, knowledge assignments, reading, resource banks, guided tours, visits to departments, films, job rotation.

PRINCIPLES AND PRACTICE OF MANAGEMENT

1. Organizational principles
2. Production planning and control
3. Financial management
4. Management services
5. Numerical studies (operations research, statistics, computers)
6. Personnel management
7. Marketing

Lectures, talks, external courses at college, etc., management games, case studies, seminars, reading assignments, coaching, under-studying.

BEHAVIOURAL STUDIES

1. Principles of human behaviour
2. Motivation
3. Group theory
4. Leadership
5. Communication
6. Attitudes and change
7. Counselling
8. Teaching and learning
9. Interviewing

Role play, group dynamics, talks, discussions, laboratory training, syndicate work, reading assignments, coaching, interactive games.

TECHNICAL AND PERSONAL SKILLS

1. Technology of own discipline
2. Report writing
3. Speaking
4. Efficient reading
5. Chairmanship
6. Question technique and listening
7. Administration of offices and paperwork

External courses, specialist tutors, correspondence courses, role play, in-tray exercises.

ENVIRONMENTAL STUDIES

1. Economic Systems
2. Relationships with government and other bodies
3. Legal Studies
4. Relationships with EEC and abroad
5. Social responsibility and ecology
6. Ethics of business
7. Public relations

Study groups, seminars, lectures, short 'acquaint' courses, reading, visits, knowledge assignments.

The Training of Supervisors and Managers

This list is by no means exhaustive and again it must be stressed that the emphasis will vary with the level of management. The choice of training strategies will be determined by time and business pressures as well as by the effectiveness of the technique, e.g. supervisory training may well be best tackled by an external course, but it could be more convenient to spend a half-day per week in-plant using formal tuition over a long period than to send the trainees away. Another factor is the necessity to balance short- and long-term instructional goals; the training required for efficient performance of the job held at this moment may well need to be extended for succession training (at the expense of job time now – often an unpopular compromise). Finally, another criterion for choice of strategy is the depth of knowledge required; some subjects may only require an acquaintance level for certain managers, but an in-depth knowledge will be needed by people who are to use the technique in their day-to-day managerial role. The ability to assess the level, depth and 'need-to-know' is one of the most valuable contributions the specialist trainer can make to management development within an organization. Much of his work will lie in advising senior line management of available strategies and resources, together with aid in identifying the training needs of their subordinates.

Chapter Sixteen

Does Your Training Work? –
Reviewing Effectiveness

Training Records

In order to assess and evaluate the efficiency of the training process it is necessary to keep accurate, up-to-date records of all training carried out. There are a number of reasons why training should be recorded:

> Historical information is necessary as memory is unreliable. The records are essential for cost comparisons, follow-up arrangements and reviews of performance before and after instruction. They also provide data for validation of a particular training technique when compared with another.
>
> It is necessary to identify training needs and potential of personnel for appraisal procedures, career development and planned succession. The matching up of jobs and people depends upon the accuracy with which their training record has been updated.
>
> Statutory requirements must be met. These include a record of induction, safety and hygiene training needing to be certificated, and information required by law.
>
> Training records meet the requirements of outside bodies such as Industrial Training Boards (for the recoupment of levy in the form of grant or to claim exemption from levy), who require a total picture of the manpower resources and the level of training of the staff.

Basically, all records should be as simple and easy to use as possible, allowing easy access and extraction of relevant details. They should also be appropriate to the needs of the business, providing relevant data to aid decision making. They must be economical in terms of cost, space and time, and easy to fill in, so that there is no demotivating irritation at the detail required. Finally, it is desirable that training records are easily integrated to fit in with other personnel records, even though recording may be carried out at many different sites, i.e. a company-wide policy of man management records is most desirable.

The types of record that are needed can be conveniently grouped into individual and summary records. Individual records need to be kept to show (a) who has completed previous training and in what subjects, (b) on what training programme or course, (c) to what level or stage and results and (d) training costs apportioned to individual (fees etc.).

This can be termed a basic record of historical information. Allied to this there will need to be a separate record kept for when that person is actually undergoing training, a form of progress report on results of assessments, tests and assignments, along with comments of trainers and other details needed to monitor the programme. This progress report can be attached to the basic report, the final details having been entered on the basic record, it can then be destroyed.

The trainers will need to keep some records of courses run, members attending, results of project work etc. if the organization is large enough to warrant a training department, together with comments of trainees and trainers on particular programmes. The follow up on this record of training results should include reactions to the results by line managers, and programme changes and amendments that follow from such reviews and notes on any special arrangements found necessary. (If the organization comes within the scope of an Industrial Training Board it is convenient to start a new page or section for each grant year.)

Financial records are most necessary in view of the training budget and the possibilities of claiming grant or exemption. The details required here are the costs involved in any piece of training:

Salaries of trainers	Overheads apportioned
Consultancy fees	to training department:
Subsistence	*Rent, Rates, Light, Heat*
Travel and fares	*etc.*

Secretarial support and
duplication

Hire charges

Cost of materials – especially
visual aids

Wages of trainees on courses,
etc.

Finally there are those records which are kept by the trainee himself. Sometimes referred to as log or check books, these records note the training and work experience gained by the trainee against a planned programme, with the trainer merely signing or initialling the correctness of the information recorded. These records are essential for peripatetic trainees, or those on a joint off-job/on-job training scheme where the work experience has to be certificated.

The design and location of the records deserve some thought and planning. Since the individual records will be expected to last throughout an employee's career, some durable material such as card is an advantage. The size of the card has to be considered and with the amount of information recorded on individual cards; anything less than A4 may be insufficient. If they are to be stored with other personnel files, it is important that they fit the folders or filing cabinets already in use. The centralization of records must be balanced with the locations of people who will make greatest use of them, people who will keep them up to date and who will be responsible for them (often a function of whether the firm has a separate Training Officer). Whoever takes charge of the records, it must be remembered that they are confidential material, containing personal reporting, so must therefore be secure. One last reiteration, no evaluation can be effective unless records are kept constantly updated with the latest position; records which are incomplete will make the next step in the review of training effectiveness almost impossible.

Evaluation of Quality of Training

After the training programme has been completed and the current training record filled in, the performance of trainees can be evaluated and the attention of the training staff drawn towards specific action for improvement, where necessary. For this purpose it is important to know whether the trainee was of the required grade for instruction, i.e. had selection been accurate, or whether the training itself is below quality.

For the former, it is necessary to have access to the original selection records early on in the training process (so that specific weaknesses can be remedied on the way) and for the latter, control graphs of the trainee's performance whilst under instruction, or some other monitoring method are necessary. Where groups of trainees have undergone the same training programme, it is helpful to have group achievement results to gain the norm.

From these results it is possible to:

> Isolate areas of difficulty and suggest strategies for overcoming them.
>
> Modify unrealistic training targets in the light of actual group performance.
>
> Determine whether motivation of trainees is of the required level, e.g. financial incentives for greater output during training.
>
> Compare initial selection to actual performance ratings.
>
> Highlight causes of absenteeism and labour turnover during training.
>
> Evaluate and modify instruction for future training programmes.

Evaluation of Training Costs

Cost benefit analysis of training is difficult since some data (e.g. labour turnover costs) are difficult to apportion accurately between selection, training, and production factors. However cost benefit figures will be the sort of information top management is looking for in its overall review of training policy and may well affect the training budget for the forthcoming financial year. Thus every effort should be made to present cost benefit analyses and savings as accurately as possible.

Shortening of training time
The real criterion of when a person is trained is the attainment of Experienced Worker Standard. If systematic training

shortens the length of time needed to reach this target, then this is a cost saving. It can be expressed as nett savings in terms of lost production as in the example in fig. 28.

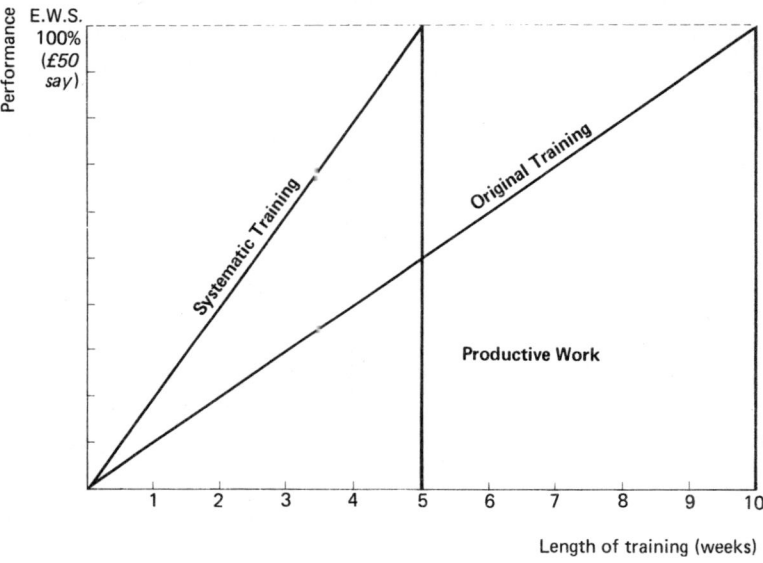

Fig. 28 Graphical representation of cost savings in terms of lost production when training time is shortened.

In the original scheme the loss to production is half of 10 weeks at an estimated £50 per week.

$$\frac{10 \times £50}{2} = £250$$

With systematic training, the training time is reduced by 50%, so the lost production now becomes

$$\frac{5 \times 50}{2} = £125$$

Thus the saving in lost production time = £250–£125 = £125 per trainee.

Does Your Training Work? – Reviewing Effectiveness

With the addition of overheads at well over 100% the real saving could amount to something nearer £400.

Another means of analysing the cost benefits of a shortening of training time is a refinement of the above method, an 'hours lost to production' basis. If the target performance is taken to be 100, comparisons of the length of time needed to reach this figure between trainees under the old system and more systematic training can be presented as in fig. 29.

Working week = 40 hours. Trainee A = old method; B = systematically trained

Weeks in trg.	Performance		Hours lost to production	
	Trainee A	Trainee B	Trainee A	Trainee B
1	20	25	$\frac{100-20\times40}{100}=32$	$\frac{100-25\times40}{100}=30$
2	45	55	$\frac{100-45\times40}{100}=22$	$\frac{100-55\times40}{100}=18$
3	60	85	$\frac{100-60\times40}{100}=16$	$\frac{100-85\times40}{100}=6$
4	85	100	$\frac{100-85\times40}{100}=6$	0
5	100		0	0
			76	54

Therefore the saving in hours lost to production is 76 − 54 hours = 22 hours at the hourly rate + overhead charge (say, £2 per hour + £3.50 per hour overheads = 2 + 3.5 × 22 = £121 per trainee).

Fig. 29 Calculation of the saving, through a shortening of training time, of hours lost to production.

Reject and scrap rate reduction
Collecting data for rejected production and scrap materials is time consuming but rewarding. Where systematic training has been installed obviously there should be an improvement in quality, so weekly figures of the amount of material wasted and the number of rejects should drop considerably. Even where no accurate data is available an assessed figure can be agreed with the departmental manager of the likely cost of scrap and rework per operator during his training period. With any reduction in training time, or any increase in quality aspects due to systematic training being installed, figures can be drawn up to show the total cost of saving. A dramatic way of showing this is to draw

Does Your Training Work? – Reviewing Effectiveness

up a table of the amount of savings that can be made with an increased number of trainees or where materials cost increases. This is shown in fig. 30.

Cost per trainee of scrap and reject work during trg period	Reduction in trg time of			
	10%	20%	30%	40%
£50	£45	£40	£35	£30
£100	£90	£80	£70	£60
£150	£135	£120	£105	£90
£200	£180	£160	£140	£120

Fig. 30   Table of savings in material and scrap through a shortening of training time.

In this example if the trainee's scrap costs during training are £200 worth of material plus rework, systematic training's ability to reduce the training time by 40% would save £80 per trainee in material costs alone.

Increase in production (volume per operator)
A simple calculation of cost benefits is possible if systematic training has increased the amount of work produced by an operator, i.e. an improvement in his skills. All that is required is the percentage increase in production × number of weeks × works cost per unit.

Increase in overhead recovery
Where training time is shortened or productivity increased by training, there is a reduction in overhead cost per unit. This saving in fixed overheads should be included in any cost benefit figures claimed for systematic training.

Costs of labour turnover during training
A simplistic way of showing the costs of labour turnover during training can be expressed as follows:

    Time spent by trainees under instruction = 1 month

    Cost of instruction (trainees wages, overheads, materials, etc.) = £600 per month

Number of trainees recruited = 20

Training cost per trainee = $\dfrac{600}{20}$ = £30

Number of trainees who left = 6

Training cost of leavers = 6 × 30 = £180 per month

However this does not present the true cost of labour turnover, since there is the loss of possible production to be taken into account as well (often a difficult assessment in monetary terms).

Cost of not training
Apart from the more obvious quantifiable aspects of training costs, a useful evaluation is to attempt to assess the loss to a company through lack of training. From experience production losses due to lack of fully trained operators, maintenance and supervisory staff can be estimated at around three working days per year. At least half of this can be attributed to poor training in the author's experience, so a simple calculation of cost of production per day multiplied by one and a half will give an average figure. (This is a cautious estimate based on fact; in some companies it was trebled.) Changes in product also bring training needs, which result in drops in efficiency when new styles are introduced if operators and supervisors react slowly through lack of training. The average time taken to achieve full production after a style change can be halved by well trained staff – a figure well worth evaluating in companies where product changes are frequent.

Recruitment of 'green' labour is easier for those companies with a recognized training scheme. It is worth while to try to quantify the rise in job appeal that accrues to the firm after systematic operator training has been installed. It is necessary at the selection interview to record this information ('Why come here?') and to abstract that proportion of new starters who nominate training as a principal recruitment feature. Another useful estimate is the cost of shortage in skills due to recruitment difficulties – not too difficult to produce!

'Bottlenecks' in production
Those places where hold-ups become a frequent feature of daily work are areas which have probably been highlighted as areas of specific training need in the original training plan. At the evaluation stage, an estimate of the costs incurred due to shortage of skills at bottleneck points, compared with the increase in rate of work-flow after training, will produce important cost benefit figures for management.

Evaluating Attitude Change

This is the most difficult evaluative process of all in the review of training. The problem lies in the ability to quantify changes in attitude before and after training. However it is essential, particularly with supervisory and management training, to have evidence of changes in approach, style and adaptability as a result of the learning process. Appraisal reports by the trainee's immediate superior are the usual tools to gauge such changes, but inevitably these tend to be subjective. Questionnaires may also be drafted pre and post training to assess differences in described attitudes, filled in by the trainee and evaluated by the training staff. However changes in the affective areas of behaviour are concerned with experiences of individual persons learning to act in their roles in the concern. It is their collective actions which make up the 'atmosphere' and keep the institution going as a corporate body. Changes in morale are definable not only as increased productivity figures but in willingness, creativity and a desire to make the firm a better place to work in. A caring company that trains its staff should notice these outward and visible signs and not be afraid to comment on non-quantifiable aspects of performance such as motivation, attitudes to work, team building and morale as a result of its commitment to training, subjective though they may be.

Conducting the Training Review

After data has been gathered, records examined, cost analyses collated, reports and appraisals furnished, there comes the

Does Your Training Work? – Reviewing Effectiveness

review of training performance. Some decisions on training reviews will have already been made at the planning phase, i.e. when the review will take place and who will carry out such an audit, but now we compare results with objectives and see how far our training needs have been met.

The best method of conducting training reviews is to formulate a questionnaire covering the main areas of training activity, and to proceed step-by-step, answering each point on the checklist in sequential order:

1. Did the board set a clear policy on its training intent?
2. Was it effectively publicized throughout the organization?
3. How much of the planned training was carried out?
4. If not, why not? (e.g. unrealistic targets, lack of suitable trainees, lack of funds, changes in personnel, external factors [such as markets decreasing in company control, etc.]).
5. What training has been (a) successful, (b) adequate or (c) unsuccessful and why?
6. What cost benefits have there been to the company through more systematic training?
7. What improvements in morale and attitudes were noticeable as a result of the training function?
8. Did allocated responsibilities for training work effectively (e.g. did line management fulfil its tutorial responsibility etc.)?
9. Were the methods and techniques employed appropriate for the learning objectives?
10. In individual programmes, what difficulties and obstacles were met at the 'transfer to production' phase?
11. What were the reactions of line management not involved in the training programme?
12. What further training needs have been discovered as a result of the training activity?
13. What non-training deficiencies have been highlighted as a result of the programme (e.g. recruitment, selection or induction problems, departmental attitudes or working methods)?

14. Was the performance of the training staff individually and corporately effective? What strengthening may it need?
15. As a result of the review what changes in training policy, procedures and budgeting will be necessary?

Needless to say, it is useless to conduct such a review unless action is taken as a result not only in the training field but also in the non-training activities which have prevented people from gaining the new skills and knowledge that were envisaged. This is why it is particularly important that top management takes part in the review process since they have sufficient 'muscle' to ensure remedial action throughout the organization. The review is the ultimate feedback mechanism in the training cycle, providing data for revision of:

>   Training policy.
>   Publication of training plans.
>   Training objectives.
>   Budgetary allocation.
>   Allocation of teaching responsibilities.
>   Use of outside consultants and courses.
>   Training methods and techniques.
>   Training department staffing.
>   Methods of reviewing training.

As such it is a most valuable managerial procedure, providing an overall view of how the organization has benefited from training, identifying successes and failures that have resulted and provided a basis for improving future training plans.

Chapter Seventeen
Administering Training

Once the training programmes have been evaluated, the cost effectiveness of the training audited and the process reviewed, it is time to write definitive procedures and strategies in the form of a training manual. All the work is brought together in one handbook, the final step in the training process, since it would be impossible to draft such a document unless a thorough evaluation had taken place.

Training Manuals

These should contain comprehensive training details for particular jobs. A balance has to be struck between too much detail on the one hand and sufficient information for the instructional team to set up, train and evaluate particular programmes on the other. Training manuals should include the following information.

Introduction
A brief introduction should explain the overall objectives, method of approach and background to the programme, to enable trainers to grasp the principles of successful interpretation of the material.

The job
This section should describe the job, specify the skills, knowledge and attitudes necessary for successful performance and outline the standards to be achieved, including instructional objectives in some detail. A guide to trainers on the analytical methods employed in designing the training is a useful addendum.

Administering Training

Selecting trainees
Essentially a personnel specification, this section should deal with standard tests to be employed at selection, instructions for scoring and administering such selection tests and general advice on the type of personality and aptitudes most likely to be successful in training for the job. Any hints on identifying applicant's areas of training need would also be included under this heading.

Organization of training
Factors here would be location of the programme, i.e. on-job training centre, local college etc., who will do the training including hints on the selection and suitability of instructors, and the budgetary resources allocated to finance the work.

Training programme
The total period of training, the regularity of its occurrence, the length of the course and its major stages and the detailed programme for the individual sessions (preferably with behavioural objectives for each one) will form the major section of the manual. A specification of the materials, tools and equipment required will also be necessary and specimen lesson plans are also included in comprehensive handbooks.

Performance monitoring and recording
Instructions on the assessment, marking and reporting of trainee's progress will need to be given. These control mechanisms will need examples of learners' graphs, daily work sheets, report forms and appraisal methods for a full operation of the scheme.

Evaluation procedures
The agreed method of evaluating the success or otherwise of the training is described fully and the strategies for providing adequate feedback to management, trainers and learners should be clearly described in simple language. From experience, cost effectiveness analyses require quite detailed instructions for their successful completion by training staff, so this section will require very careful drafting.

When it is completed the training manual or handbook forms a complete guide to the whole process, so care should be taken to ensure that it is as comprehensive as possible and regularly updated as changes in procedures evolve with the passage of time.

Organization of Training

Responsibility and corresponding authority for the training function need to be clearly defined throughout the organization. In small companies, training is generally of the on-job type conducted by line management, often under the general direction of the personnel department. Line management has a vested interest in training, since output, money, prestige and a stable labour force are much affected by the amount of effort put into the training function departmentally. The line manager has therefore to ensure that his labour force is adequately trained, even though he may not carry out much of the actual instruction himself. He must however be able to identify his subordinates' training needs, recognize where their 'gaps' will fill organizational requirements, set performance standards and instructional objectives necessary to attain them, decide the methods of training that will reach such targets and be able to evaluate the success of the training effort of his department.

In slightly larger companies, the burden of being a trainer-manager may mean that a degree of delegation has to be introduced. For instance, a manager can delegate training to a subordinate who is a specialist in some other field (such as method study, employee relations or quality control). However training is usually a 'poor relation' to the specialist's first calling, and can be neglected, since the only aspects of training that can be delegated are determining the methods of instruction and actually carrying out the instruction. (The determination of objectives, standards, targets and training needs will still lie in the hands of the line manager.)

Perhaps a better solution is the appointment of a training officer, subordinate to the line manager. Such a position is likely to include the following duties in his job description:

Administering Training

> Assisting the manager to formulate training plans.
>
> Analysis of knowledge, skills and attitudes required in particular posts.
>
> Assisting in formulating training objectives and programmes.
>
> Setting targets and performance standards.
>
> Carrying out instruction, or training instructional personnel.
>
> Arranging suitable monitoring devices for the assessment of training performance.
>
> Providing an up-to-date information service on training available outside the company.
>
> Administering detail arrangements for off-job courses.
>
> Keeping records of all kinds of training carried out for the training review.

It will be seen from the above that the training officer provides a service to the line manager of an advisory and consultancy nature, and does not remove from that manager the overall responsibility for training. What power the training officer has is delegated to him and carried out under the authority of the line manager, a fact often misconstrued in the small to medium sized company, where role conflict can occur between the manager and his training officer due to differences in perception of status by production staff.

The vast majority of large organizations have a separate training function, with a specialist manager, though it may be linked to other human resources such as personnel or employee relations. Ideally, it should have its own training director and at least a say at top management level through a personnel director. The department has a staff function, i.e. it provides specialist input to line management in the main area of programme formulation, advice, service and control. It has a similar list of duties to the training officer, but more broadly based throughout the organization including:

> Identification of training needs at all levels.

Administering Training

Formulation of plans and objectives in line with training policy.

Assignment of instructional responsibilities.

Training programme design in consultation with line management.

Collection and preparation of training media and learning resources (materials, curricula, visual aids, outlines, forms, trainee notes etc.).

Administration of courses in-plant, and instruction where necessary.

Oversight of apprentice and registered trainee programmes (co-ordination of on-job/off-job aspects).

Management development to level specified by training policy.

Training of trainers (line personnel and instructors).

Monitoring and control mechanisms sufficient for effective evaluation or training.

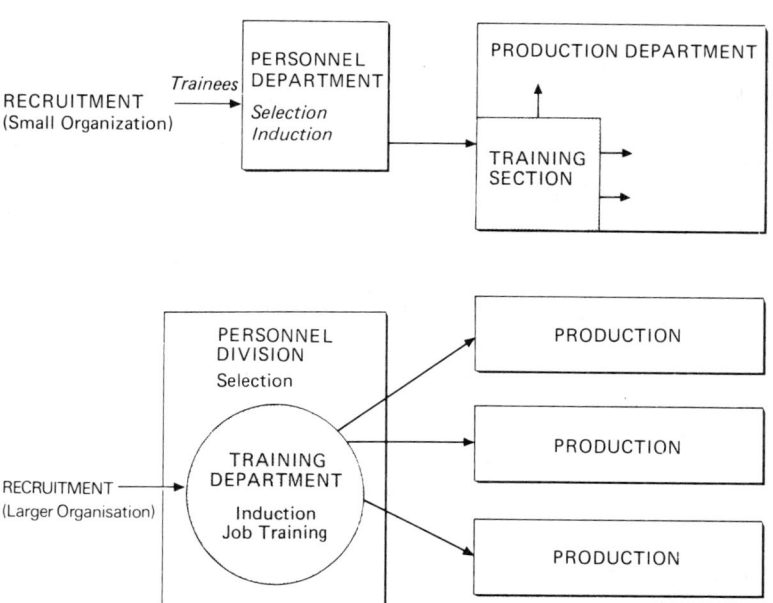

Fig. 31 Model depicting change of location of training department with growth.

Administering Training

The difference between the two set-ups can be seen diagrammatically as a model in fig. 31 which clearly shows the autonomy of such a department with its attendant advantages of overview, but inescapable divorce from the work force.

The training of sales staff tends generally to be delegated to the marketing and sales division, since the job specifications for such people require different emphases during training. There is a sound argument however for allowing training specialists to examine the social skills needed from an analytical point of view as the expertise in teaching such skills may not exist within the marketing function.

Selection and Training of Trainers

On-job trainers and instructors
On-job trainers are people who instruct in the working situation whilst the trainee is engaged in the day-to-day work of a unit or department. In many cases the requirements of an on-job trainer are fault correction and maintenance of standards after initial training has been given. Where very limited skills are involved or where staff already possess the basic skills of the job, the on-job trainer's role consists of coaching, giving hints or tips based on experience and correcting performance. They may give short pieces of instruction based upon tasks which have already been analysed and where programmes have been well validated together with the attendant manuals and training aids. Basically however, they are part-time trainers whose duties include some instructional work, especially when changes in product or routine are minor enough not to warrant a complete new training programme.

On-job trainers must know:

> All the key jobs with the department.
> Faults likely to be recurrent for new trainees.
> Acceptable standards of performance and quality.
> The 'trainable moment' and how to use such opportunities wisely and well.
> Sufficient instructional technique to be able to communicate correct working methods on simple tasks.

Administering Training

The old Training Within Industry (TWI) Job Instruction course forms an excellent basis for the on-job trainer. This course, run in industry on lines sponsored by the Ministry of Labour during World War Two, is still good ground work and includes job breakdown (a simple form of analysis), how to instruct and how to put trainees to work. Two or three days is usual for such courses, though refinements such as the use of visual aids, the keeping of simple records and two or three role play assessed demonstrations make five days a more realistic and satisfactory training period for the new on-job trainer. The emphasis in such courses, whether run internally or off the job, is a sound basis in common sense routines, simple use of non-technical language and a strong bias towards active learning situations.

Instructors
This training requires a syllabus of more depth and detail, since quite often the instructor is a full-time trainer, conducting teaching sessions both on- and off-job, with responsibilities that include teaching theoretical knowledge as well as skills and attitudes. He may have to instruct groups of trainees during such sessions, so care must be taken to draft a job description which covers communicating skills. The selection of such a person for training should include the following criteria:

> How much of the person's time will be spent on actual instruction?
> To whom will the instructor be responsible?
> What proportions of his training will be spent on teaching knowledge sessions to groups as opposed to skills to individuals?
> With whom will the instructor need to liaise?
> What temperament and personality fits the role best?
> Who will monitor the instructor's performance?
> What technical qualifications and experience must he/she possess?
> How is the instructor to be recruited, e.g. recommendation, volunteering, advertisements?

Administering Training

>Who carries out selection?
>
>If this is an internal appointment, how do we 'sell' the change of role?
>
>At what salary point and level in the company hierarchy will the new instructor be placed?

After selection, a decision must be taken on the way in which the person can acquire knowledge, skills and attitudes necessary for the post. A new instructor has the opportunity of learning his job from existing instructors within the firm, by attending an outside course or by coaching from his superior. Ideally, the new trainer should benefit from a combination of all three inputs since this will give him a frame of reference from which he can view the whole field of training. His job description will probably cover a wider area than that of the on-job trainer, including:

>Recognition of training needs.
>
>Analysis (up to an agreed level) of jobs and tasks.
>
>Drafting of job descriptions.
>
>Deciding on job specifications (knowledge skills and attitudes to be learnt).
>
>Awareness of learning theory, specifically related to tasks within the firm.
>
>Aiding in setting objectives and planning training programmes for specific levels of staff.
>
>Application of instructional strategies to meet training needs.
>
>Planning, preparing and giving instruction.
>
>Familiarity with training aids and equipment and their appropriateness for teaching strategies.
>
>Monitoring and recording trainees' performance.
>
>Assessing and evaluation of training carried out at a preliminary level.

Training officers
The term 'training officer' is an inexact description. As has been discussed earlier the job of a training officer depends on

the amount of training staff and the elaboration of the set-up. The job description of a typical training officer has already been outlined, but it is convenient at this point to add the responsibilities for developing the company's training policy, and helping line management to maximize their instructional role. The personnel specification would call for a person with a degree or equivalent qualification preferably in the human resource field, at least seven years of suitable industrial experience (with line responsibility a must) and some period in training/education. Membership of the Institute of Training Officers or Personnel Management, even at graduate level, shows an early commitment to the training world, but some form of professional association is invaluable.

The particular aptitudes one would look for, as well as a desire to manage learning situations, are a 'gestalt' overview of policy formation, the ability to think creatively about organizational development, a clear understanding of interactive behaviour in working groups and an analytical approach to programme design. In a larger set-up, the need to manage a department and ability to administer the effective use of resources is important.

In addition to the above general knowledge requirements, a training officer will need to know something about the products of the organization, well enough to be able to recognize skill shortages. If previous experience in the industry is not specified at recruitment (and there are good reasons for introducing outside experience in training processes since, after all, the principles of training are the same across all organizations) then the new training officer will rapidly need to acquire detailed knowledge of the company and its products. For this reason many new training officers are allowed an orientation period, getting to know the management, shop stewards, company communication patterns, production problems etc. Many human resource managers at director level feel that a splendid way to orientate a new training officer is to get him to submit his proposals for meeting training needs in the form of a written report as early as possible in his new career. This will show the directorate how the new trainer has assimilated tricky areas of his work, such as how far the training organization impinges on

Administering Training

line managers training responsibilities and the degree of training activity within various parts of the firm, allied to the personalities that head up each section.

Experienced training officers will usually have a wide knowledge not only of training procedures but of the problems of tailoring learning experiences to fit the organizational profile. However the newly appointed training officer may well need an advanced course or seminar to help him. In addition to the basic four to six week training officers' course certain higher education centres run specialist short courses on specific areas of the training process. An up-to-date list of such courses, together with consultants in the field, advisory bodies and other relevant information should be kept by all organizations. Works of reference, such as the Personnel and Training Management Yearbook and Directory (Kogan-Page), are essential in any resource bank set up to cover this area.

The training officer should also be encouraged, as a developmental policy, to forge links with colleagues in other organizations and to maintain close contact with local and national colleges and educational institutions, especially universities engaged in research and professional bodies with training responsibilities. A requirement of the work is to keep up-to-date with new concepts in the human resourcing field (an example might be Transactional Analysis as a training aid) and by conducting as much experimental work as is possible within the organization.

The new training officer may need to be trained in self-presentation techniques, since much of his work will be in a 'selling' role, presenting training policies to often half-convinced line management and persuading them to fulfil their training responsibilities (such as the release of key personnel for development). To this end he will need to be well versed in social skills, straightforward in manner and able to gain respect for his professional ability to deliver the goods. Since much of his work will be in transacting with other managers, a good grounding in applied psychology will almost certainly be an item on the training officer's job specification.

In September 1976, the then TSA (now the Training Services Division of the Manpower Services Commission) set up a committee with the following terms of reference: 'To consider the roles, relationships, training needs and current training of those staff who have specific responsibilities for training and to make recommendations on

(a) the pattern of training required for such staff
(b) the provision of such training
(c) the appropriate means of its evaluation, oversight and approval.'

As a result, two working parties were formed to look at (a) the roles and competency of training staff and (b) resources, methods and standards. Their joint report formed the basis of a discussion document, which led to the Training of Trainers Committee issuing the following recommendations in a report called *The Training of Trainers* (MSC, price £2.50):

1. Organizations should be encouraged to review the allocation of training responsibilities and their selection and development of training staff. Industrial Training Boards should be encouraged to include these matters in their exemption criteria (for notes on the Manpower Services Commission, TSA and Industrial Training Boards, see next chapter).

2. Those concerned with the education and training of managerial, professional, trade union and other staff should be encouraged to consider how an understanding of the role such staff can play in training may be more effectively included in these programmes.

3. Training staff should be capable of understanding and fitting into the business or organizational environment in which they work as well as understanding the appropriate training technology, and if necessary receive training in these aspects.

4. The concept of Introductory Training Officers' Courses should be dropped and replaced by that of a range of core-competency programmes geared to the requirements and circumstances of those participating and meeting a common Code of Practice.

5. The Manpower Services Commission should liaise closely with the Institute of Personnel Management and the Institute of Training Officers in working through with them the

relationship between core competency training and the professional qualifications which are rightly the prerogative and responsibility of these bodies.

6. Organizations wishing to set up their own form of accreditation for individuals completing particular core competency programmes should be encouraged to do so. It is, however, neither feasible nor desirable that a common national scheme of individual accreditation be established at this time.

7. The Manpower Services Commission should set up a scheme whereby any organization willing to comply with the Code of Practice in relation to core-competency programmes for training staff should be able voluntarily to register, and derive certain benefits from doing so.

8. Any core-competency programmes which the Manpower Services Commission itself may sponsor or financially support should be expected to meet the requirements for registration.

9. Those who train training staff should themselves have personal development plans. The Manpower Services Commission should ensure that continuing provision is made for workshops, seminars etc. for these staff.

10. An increased provision of relevant research and development activities should be encouraged and results made more widely known; so that positive benefits can be derived.

11. The possibility of setting up a Chair of Training at a British university or equivalent body should be investigated further.

12. A National Advisory Group should be set up to oversee and co-ordinate the continuing development of the training of training staff, and to review progress. It should be supported where appropriate by a network of informal groups and activities.

From the foregoing recommendations, it is plain to see that the Training of Trainers Committee is concerned about the credibility and effectiveness of professional trainers. Though competence in training techniques is essential, wider horizons are necessary if training officers are to make a greater contribution to the overall objectives of the organization. The committee's views on what it considers to be common areas of know-how in core competencies make very interesting reading:

1. The organization and its business
   Training staff should have a sufficient understanding for their job needs of:
   The structure, objectives and policies.
   The products or services.
   The business environment and practices.
   The technology and work processes.
   The relationships, needs and problems of their own organizations.
   The way organizations work and develop.

2. The training function and specialist roles
   They should have a sufficient understanding of:
   How training is and may be organized effectively.
   Trainer roles, what influences these in practice in their organization, and how these may be appropriately extended and developed.
   Relationships with education and training resources inside and outside the organization and how these may be used.

3. Learning and the design of learning
   They should have a sufficient understanding of:
   How, where, when and why others learn.
   The various ways in which people can be helped to learn in practice, e.g. off- or on-the-job, by specific training activities or by self development through work and experience.
   Different approaches to designing, implementing and evaluating learning and learning systems.

4. Diagnosis and problem solving
   They should have a sufficient understanding of:
   Appropriate systems and methods of diagnosing situations.
   How problems and opportunities present themselves.
   How learning needs and priorities may be identified.
   What is involved by way of judgement, strategy and tactics in arriving at practicable solutions and getting them implemented.

5. People in organizations
   They should have a sufficient understanding of:
   Their own and others' needs and behaviour as individuals

and groups and how this affects learning and the day-to-day relationships of the trainer.
Ways of handling these relationships in practice.
Relevant skills of advocacy, selling, communication, advising, coaching etc.

In addition to these common know-how areas, the committee felt that training staff require specific knowledge and skills in four 'role elements' which can be used as a framework for establishing key abilities in different jobs. The four areas are (a) a direct training element, i.e. the training techniques involved in preparing for and carrying out direct tuition, (b) a planning and organizing element to provide a framework for the activities of an organization, (c) a determining or managing element which is characterized by the exercise of effective structural power at a policy influencing level and (d) a consulting and advisory element.

These important recommendations by the Manpower Services Commission Training of Trainers Committee will obviously result in considerable progress being made in this field in the near future and a further report on the training of 'direct' trainers (those in face-to-face situations, e.g. instructors, on-job trainers etc.) is promised.

The major concern for all training of training staff should be that such specialists are credible and effective in the great variety of roles and settings in which they operate. Only thus will the standards of professionalism and the organizational status of trainers be raised to the level at which they have a real say in the formation of policy as a right and not as a poor relation of the personnel department invited for the occasion.

Chapter Eighteen
Training Agencies, Associations and Information

Government Agencies
Trainers in industry will need to know about the government agencies that administer the Employment and Training Act 1973 and its forerunner the Industrial Training Act 1964. Under the former Act, the Manpower Services Commission was set up with its two executive arms, one the Training Services Agency (TSA) and the other the Employment Services Agency (ESA).

Manpower Services Commission
This is an independently operating commission established on 1st January 1974, responsible to the Secretary of State for Employment. The ten man commission has representatives from employers, trade unions, local authorities and educational interests. Broadly, their function is to implement policies laid down by the Secretary of State for Employment and voted by Parliament, but it also advises on the formulation of such policy and makes its own public pronouncements on the training and employment situation. The MSC has a full-time chairman (the other nine members being part-time), with a director and in consultation with the Secretary of State formulates a five-year plan for manpower planning and training, taking into account recent developments and forecasts in the fields of education and the national economic position.

Training Services Agency
This is a statutory body responsible to the Manpower Services Commission. It is controlled by a chief executive and his deputy and (a) oversees and co-ordinates the work of the Industrial Training Boards (see later paragraph), (b) promotes training

Training Agencies, Associations and Information

where necessary in industries and organizations not covered by the ITBs, (c) responds to training needs of particular industries, particularly where there is a strong national interest in doing so, (d) promotes research and development into training practices, and (e) runs two particular schemes – the Training Opportunities Scheme (TOPS) and Training Within Industry (TWI) mentioned earlier.

In 1977, fifteen million people were employed in firms covered by the Industrial Training Boards, out of a total working population of twenty-five million. However, many of the latter would be working in nationalized industries which have a statutory obligation to provide effective training.

On 1st April 1978, the TSA became the Training Services Division of the MSC.

Employment Services Agency

This, the other arm responsible to the MSC operates in a similar fashion to the TSA, but in the field of national public employment. It provides career guidance, special services for the disabled, job opportunities in other parts of the country and advises on retraining for different skills. It runs local employment offices and Jobcentres, the Occupational Guidance Scheme, the Professional and Executive Register (PER) and the Employment Transfer Scheme amongst other duties. However, since the scope of this book does not include personnel and employment practices, further details can be found elsewhere.

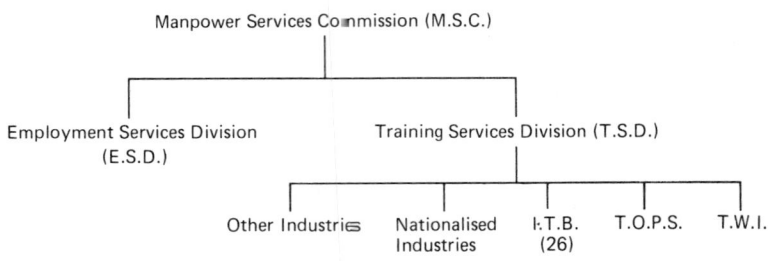

Fig. 32 Hierarchy of government training organizations.

On 1st April 1978 the ESA was retitled the Employment Services Division of the MSC.

To recapitulate, the statutory training set up looks like the diagram in fig. 32.

Industrial Training Boards
Originally set up under the Industrial Training Act 1964 and modified by the Employment and Training Act 1973, the twenty-six Industrial Training Boards report to the Training Services Agency.

The ITBs' tasks are to promote the importance of good training to management, to aid this by increasing the number of trainers and raising instructional standards, to forecast training needs and draw up recommendations for ensuring a supply of trained labour to meet the needs of the particular industry and to work to develop and maintain standards of industrial training by implementing these recommendations. They also implement the requirements of the Acts in respect of spreading the cost of training, since a system of financial inducements was established by which the employer is presented with a choice between training and contributing towards the costs of the employers who do train. Exemptions from the levy can be gained by those firms who are deemed by the Board to be meeting their own training needs. A certificate to this effect is issued by the Board concerned and may be effective for one, two or three years, being withdrawn if the employer fails to meet requirements.

Specific grants for training in key activity areas are also available (Key Training Activities being so designated by the Board and the MSC) and, should the majority of employers in an industry wish it, grants for specific training needs can be raised by a levy of all firms, even those with exemption certificates, to meet this request. Financial help is also available for firms participating in Group Training Schemes in their early formative years, where associations of small firms employ a training officer and spread his duties amongst them. The benefits of such groupings are obvious; however these schemes are expected to become self supporting in time.

Training Agencies, Associations and Information

Most boards operate on a regional structure, based on geographical areas, and have regional, senior and local training advisers implementing board policy. Larger training boards have training centres staffed by the board, teaching craft and technician skills in the main. Other board staff may include training officers of Group Training Schemes, referred to above, where the board itself employs the trainer and recoups costs from the scheme. Staff of the ITBs have a dual role of watchdog and tutor which in practice requires considerable human relations skill as well as a deep knowledge of training practices, in order to achieve the high standards of personal example necessary in such work.

Training Opportunities Scheme (TOPS)
This scheme, created in 1972 and superseding the old Vocational Training Scheme, is aimed at providing retraining opportunities, particularly for the mature worker, where their skills have become obsolete, not locally applicable or simply because they need a change. Most TOPS training is carried out in what are known as Skillcentres (formerly Government Training Centres), but training available under TOPS has recently extended to white collar and management skills and this has meant that the TSD has hired places at colleges, business schools, polytechnics and universities.

The scheme allows both employed and unemployed workers to apply for places under TOPS and qualify for allowances during training. These allowances are geared to the cost of living and are tax free, and there is also a TOPS-sponsored scheme whereby free training for workers is provided whilst still in full employment with a company. The scheme has proved popular; the numbers of people receiving TOPS training has jumped from 18,400 in 1971 to over 80,000 by 1977. There has been a marked increase in the number of TOPS training places hired in further and higher education, and in firms' training establishments, though the emphasis is still on the provision of traditional semi-skilled training, particularly for engineering and construction workers. Skillcentres, staffed by TSA trainers, are based in large centres of employment in most areas of the UK, organized on a regional basis, the most modern of which

Training Agencies, Associations and Information

are often sited in industrial estates giving workers the 'feel' of active participation in a realistic working environment. At the other end of the spectrum, TOPS courses for specialist executive skills are run at Management Centres in the higher education sector, again giving the trainee an appropriate environment in which to learn.

Training Within Industry (TWI)

During World War Two, when labour resources were stretched as never before, the then Ministry of Labour realized that, if people were to learn quickly and correctly the new skills that were required by the war effort, greater emphasis would have to be placed on instructional technique. In the USA a scheme of systematic training for supervisors had proved successful and it was imported under the title of Training Within Industry.

The topic covered, in addition to 'Job Instruction', centred on supervisory skills in the fields of human relations, safe working and improvement in work methods, and provided a sound basic knowledge with some opportunity to practise skills. They were short (around thirty hours), run either in-company or at Government premises, and have survived to this day with some modifications and additions. The TSD now operate the scheme with their own trainers and subjects covered are:

Job Methods
Job Safety
Job Relations
Office Supervisors
Retail Supervisors   } all thirty hours.
Hospital Supervisors
Operator Instructors
Clerk Instructors

There is also a two week course for people from industrial firms who are trained to become TWI trainers in their own companies. Recent developments have included shop stewards courses and export office procedure.

Voluntary Training Organizations

British Association for Commercial and Industrial Education (BACIE)
BACIE is a voluntary organization which promotes all aspects of vocational education and training, across the whole spectrum of industrial learning. It is registered as an educational charity and was founded in 1919. It played a prominent part in bringing the Industrial Training Act 1964 on to the statute book by acting as a pressure group. BACIE membership can be as an individual or as an organization and members include nationalized industries, industrial and commercial companies, education establishments, trade unions, professional bodies and associations, and national and local government departments.

Services to members include short courses and seminars on specific training and educational topics, national and regional conferences and meetings, publications over a wide range of training topics and specific contributions in the furtherance of instructional techniques. There is also the *BACIE Journal*, a monthly publication of great value to trainers, and a library service which contains a most comprehensive collection of training books and documents.

The Industrial Society
This promotes the fullest involvement of all people in their work with the aims of increasing job satisfaction for the individual and the effectiveness of organizations. It is an independent self financing voluntary organization specializing in what might be termed the human resource area – industrial relations, personnel management, communication, leadership and delegation, conditions of employment, industrial participation and the development of employees. Like BACIE, its membership is drawn from a wide spectrum of companies, nationalized industries, central and local government departments etc. It runs a consultancy service (available to members and non-members) on a variety of behavioural topics, produces a famous series of pamphlets called 'Notes for Managers', as well as many other publications invaluable to the professional

trainer and has a wide selection of films, tape-slide programmes and cassettes.

Professional Associations

The Institute of Personnel Management (IPM)
Founded more than sixty years ago, the IPM is formed of qualified and practising personnel and training managers and has forty branches in various parts of the country. Membership is open on an individual basis by examination and experience to those engaged in personnel, or specialisms such as education and training, and the grades are Fellowship (FIPM), Member (MIPM) and Associate (AMIPM). Services to members include national and branch meetings, information and library services, the monthly magazine *Personnel Management*, a wide range of publications at reduced rates, seminars and conferences and of course the value of membership as a qualification. Classes for IPM examinations are held on a part-time basis in most large regional colleges for those with appropriate entry qualifications.

The Institution of Training Officers (ITO)
As its name suggests this is a professional association of practising, qualified training officers, whose aim is to promote the science and practice of training and to set and maintain high standards of competence for trainers. It has branches throughout Great Britain and there are two grades of corporate membership – Fellow (FITO) and Member (MITO). Included in its many services to trainers are free copies of the magazine *Training* and branch meetings on training and educational topics.

Chapter Nineteen

Recapitulation

Readers will remember, it is hoped, from the chapter on planning instruction that one of the main purposes of the conclusion phase is a check on the achievement of objectives. Consolidation or revision may then take place since the amount of material passing from short- to long-term memory can be assessed. Readers are invited to use this last chapter as a refresher on the earlier work. The major use, however, of the checklist approach is in the drafting of questionnaires to aid systematic management of the training function. There follows a number of such checklists with the dual objectives referred to above, and the additional one of providing a guide to trainers on the way in which such questionnaires may be designed to fit their own situations. Each chapter will have a number of questions designed both to test recall and to promote awareness of the actual training situation as it exists currently within the trainer's own organization.

Training policy
(a) What is the definition of training?
(b) What problems may arise from training by exposure?
(c) What benefits can accrue (a) to the organization and (b) to the employee from the introduction of more systematic training?
(d) What is the total wage bill for your organization for the last financial year?
(e) How much of this is payable in levy to an Industrial Training Board?
(f) Does the formulation of training policy start at board level? Who is responsible for the overall implementation of such policies?

Recapitulation

(g) Are all line managers aware of their role as trainers within their own departments? Is it written into their job descriptions?

(h) How are training decisions taken at board level publicized throughout the organization? Is the system working properly?

(i) What feedback from last term's training performance is relevant in the formation of this term's policy?

(j) Is sufficient information of the right kind available for decisions concerning training policy? If not, what redesign of the monitoring system is necessary?

Assessing and forecasting training needs

(a) What is a training need? Define it accurately.

(b) What types of training need occur typically in organizations of all kinds?

(c) What training needs has your organization in each of the categories mentioned above?

(d) What questions does the training analyst need to ask to gain sufficient information for his analysis? Of whom?

(e) How else can information on training needs be collected?

(f) What is the Training Forecast? How is it drawn up from the training needs analysis?

(g) What information should a training forecast contain?

(h) How are the cost estimates and benefits of such training obtained in your organization? Are they accurate?

(i) Can all the training required be provided from within the organization? If not, what outside help will be needed?

(j) What is the next step in planning training systematically?

How trainees learn

(a) Incoming stimuli are received and transmitted to the brain by the senses. Which senses are involved mostly in your own trainees' learning?

(b) What is kinaesthesis? Describe some instances where it reveals itself in your working situation.

Recapitulation

(c) Why is perception important during learning? What factors can affect the levels of perception of your trainees?

(d) What is meant by the effector process?

(e) What, in your environment, helps trainees to learn?

(f) What factors in your organization hinder trainees' learning?

(g) What is 'transfer' as applied to the learning process and how can the trainer help to minimize transfer problems in the real life situation?

(h) How can the trainer inculcate correct work habits in his trainees?

(i) In skill pick-up, what is a plateau on a learning curve? Where do such plateaux occur in your own trainees' learning situations?

(j) What important factors will you bear in mind when you are designing training programmes as a result of your study of the learning process?

Why trainees learn

(a) What are intrinsic rewards as applied to trainees? What extrinsic rewards does your company offer? Do they work?

(b) What needs are satisfied at work as a general rule? What needs are left unsatisfied, in your working environment, at all levels of the organization?

(c) What incentives to greater effort are within the jurisdiction of the trainer?

(d) What factors affect the trainer/trainee relationship? How do you rate as a model?

(e) How can we reduce anxiety during learning for our trainees? What particular facets of working life are likely to make your own trainees apprehensive?

(f) What learning problems may there be for the older worker? How can you combat them?

(g) How do trainees measure their progress under your training schemes? What could you do to increase motivation during training?

(h) How can you find out the goals of each of your learners? What process already exists for such counselling?
(i) How can you possibly motivate people in your organization who are learning routine, mundane tasks?
(j) How, by your behaviour as a trainer, can you induce positive attitudes in your trainees? How do you gauge your success?

Planning training
(a) From the training forecast, a training plan is drawn up. What information should such a training plan contain? How does this compare with your firm's current planning?
(b) The training programme can be presented in columnar form. What five headings must such a programme show?
(c) How can one maintain flexibility in training programme design to cater for the various learning rates of trainees?
(d) How does one build stamina during skill type training?
(e) In your organization, how do you ensure that programmed training is actually carried out?

Analysing Jobs
(a) What is the difference between a job, a duty and a task? Are you in line with standard nomenclature (cf. *A Glossary of Training Terms*, HMSO) within your company?
(b) What is job analysis? How is it carried out in your own set-up?
(c) What are the headings on a job description? Have your employees got job descriptions? How often are they updated and by whom?
(d) What is a task list and where does it fit into the analytical process? Are your task lists currently accurate?
(e) What is the difference between a job description and a job specification? Is everyone who should appreciate this difference really clear about the uses of the two documents? If not, what should you do about it?

Recapitulation

Analysing tasks
(a) Knowledge analysis falls into two main categories, company knowledge and task knowledge. What should be included under each heading, and how do trainees in your organization actually receive such knowledge?
(b) Skill can be analysed in three stages. What headings are used for each stage, and what factors would make you chose one as opposed to another? Relate this to the level of detail needed in your company; are you using the right stage?
(c) What are the particular advantages of task analysis to the instructor? And to the trainee?
(d) Why is liaison between the training department and the method study section important? Is there a good working relationship in your outfit?
(e) Draw a diagram showing the overall relationship between job analysis, job description, job specification, knowledge and skill analysis (tasks). Does this flow actually exist in your training department?

Preparing to instruct – written work
(a) Why is it important to frame instructional objectives in behavioural terms? Do you use behavioural objectives for the sessions that you instruct back at work?
(b) In drafting session plans, what are the three major stages of teaching strategy?
(c) Describe several ways of creating student interest during the commencement phase of a session. How do you gain attention and impact prior to instruction in your current teaching?
(d) In the core of the lesson, what points are always 'must knows' for a trainee? How do you accommodate these in your session plan?
(e) How can you plan to allow students the maximum amount of participation during knowledge-type instruction? How can you test whether information has been absorbed in the conclusion phase of such lessons?

Recapitulation

Preparing to instruct – displays and visual aids
(a) What are the critical factors in deciding whether to make a pre-prepared display summary or to build one up progressively as the session develops?
(b) When would you use a whiteboard or magnetic board as opposed to a blackboard and, conversely, when is it more appropriate to use the chalkboard? What boards are available in your own training set-up? Are they suitable for the students you intend to train?
(c) What projected aids are there available to the trainer? What are the factors that you would take into account if funds were made available to choose just one piece of equipment in your real-life situation?
(d) Charts are a useful visual aid to back-up instruction. What types are there and how might you obtain or produce them?
(e) CCTV has immense potential for certain training situations. What are they and how would you justify the considerable expense concerned with such equipment?
(f) How can on-job training aids be improvised creatively at the work face?

Choosing the right method
(a) The lecture is still a feature of knowledge-type instruction. When would you use it in the working situation and why?
(b) Define (a) a seminar, (b) a tutorial and (c) a lesson. Do people get mixed up with these terms in your organization? How can you remedy this?
(c) Of what use are discussion groups as a learning experience? How would you chair a controlled group discussion?
(d) Role play has been labelled as 'a dangerous training technique'. Why is this? Think how you could use it to teach social skills in your company.
(e) What strategy would you use to teach (a) a psychomotor skill, (b) supervisory problem solving and (c) clerical and desk work?

Do-it-yourself learning
(a) Active, student-centred learning situations are very popu-

Recapitulation

lar at the moment. Why is this? Are there occasions when you could make more use of such strategies in your work?

(b) What is the trainer's role in programmed instruction – or has he been replaced? What teaching material is programmed in your own company? Should it be extended?

(c) Construct an algorithm that you could employ to advantage as a training tool.

(d) Trainees are particularly sensitive about criticism of project work and assignments. Why is this? Where could knowledge assignments help your hard-pressed trainers and benefit the trainee at the same time?

(e) In group work, the trainer is often more concerned with 'process' than 'content'. Define process and explain how feedback on process during group dynamics can aid the trainee.

Instructional technique

(a) The use of voice is most important during training sessions. What are the main points to watch when speaking formally to students? Have you practised with a tape recorder? If so how long ago?

(b) What is crucial about manner, appearance and eye contact whilst instructing? How do you match up to these principles?

(c) Why do we use questions when teaching? Draft teaching questions at the rate of one per minute for your next instruction and note the increase in participation.

(d) Do you allow fellow trainers to give you constructive feedback on your training sessions? If not, why not try it?

(e) When using boards as display summaries, list the 'dos' and 'don'ts' for instructors.

(f) How can trainees take away material for further reference from your training sessions? Justify the choice that you make in your present training (and perhaps consider alternatives).

(g) In skill-type demonstration, a traditional approach to the strategy is to refer to 'the four Ps'. What are they?

Recapitulation

(h) Are session plans, used by different instructors in your organization, available to other trainers for reference? Why not have common session plans?

(i) How do you maintain interest in knowledge (theory) sessions? How can you tell if in fact you have the attention and interest of your trainees?

(j) How can you check that your students have really learned from your session rather than have just listened? How do you and your fellow trainers obtain feedback on your own performance?

Monitoring performance and correcting faults

(a) The interval of time between error and fault correction is important in instilling correct habits during skill training. How can we ensure that this interval is kept as short as possible? How quickly is feedback obtained by trainees in your organization?

(b) Performance graphs can be expressed in many ways. Describe two types and justify your preference.

(c) How do you design progress charts for your trainees at present? What other ways could you use?

(d) What is meant by the mnemonic FACERAP in faults training?

(e) How does a faults diagnosis differ from a faults analysis? Sketch a format suitable for such a document. Do the Quality Control people in your organization have any say in fault training?

Training Supervisors and Managers

(a) Why has staff appraisal such a large part to play in developing managers? What are the results of your staff appraisal scheme, if any? Does the training department get adequate feedback of individual's training needs?

(b) What is meant by 'coaching'? What does the successful coach do? Do you coach your subordinates successfully? (Ask them!)

(c) What training needs are common to all supervisors? What training strategies have you available to meet each need?

Recapitulation

   (d) What subject matter would you include under 'company knowledge' in a training programme for new managers? Who, in fact, orientates new managers in your concern? Is it well done?

   (e) What are the benefits of establishing a recognized management centre for staff training? When would you consider buying in expertise in specialist fields?

Does your training work?

   (a) Why do we need to record training? What criteria would you use in designing basic training records?

   (b) What information will you require from financial records of training undertaken? How do you retrieve this data?

   (c) How do you ensure that training records of subordinates are available to line managers?

   (d) How can you present cost benefit analyses to back up a case for systematic training schemes?

   (e) How can you evaluate changes in attitude as a result of training?

   (f) The training review can be presented in questionnaire format. Outline at least ten of the fifteen steps in the checklist used in this book. How does your own training review compare?

Administering training

   (a) Name five headings you would expect to see in a training manual. Who is responsible for the production and up-dating of training manuals in your organization?

   (b) List the main duties of a training unit within a medium to large size company.

   (c) Describe the work of the on-job trainer and the instructor. Outline their training needs and evaluate how well these are met at present in your working situation.

   (d) What are considered to be areas of 'core competency' in the role of training officer? How do you choose and train your own senior trainers? How do you evaluate their professionalism?

(e) Does your training administration have representation at director level? Within the concern, does training have a good 'image'? How do you know? If not, what could be done to improve its public relations?

Training organizations
(a) Draw an organization chart showing the links between the Manpower Services Commission and your local ITB training adviser. What services are provided by the Training Services Division of the MSC?
(b) What is TOPS and how could you in industry become associated with the scheme?
(c) TWI has an important role in supervisory training. How could TWI Job Instruction be installed in your concern?
(d) What does BACIE do and how could you join? What are the Industrial Society's specialisms? How could you use their expertise?
(e) Name two professional associations that cater for trainers and some of their services that might prove useful to you.

A Last Word

The trainer seeks to impart a semi-permanent change in behaviour with a specific purpose. In working towards his objectives, he will learn much about an organization, its strengths and weaknesses, its people and its climate. The professional trainer will have not only a sound knowledge of training techniques and a deep understanding of how the set-up works, but will act as a catalyst for change within the whole concern. His analytical activities may expose old sores, yet his enthusiasm can pervade an entire firm. His is a very special position, giving as it does an overview of the entire working pattern and revealing much about the characters who operate it.

The trainer can help the organization in its constant need to adapt to its environment, but only if he recognizes his responsibilities as well as his opportunities. To achieve this he will need a firm grounding in ethics, and an adult sense of judge-

Recapitulation

ment. Feedback must go through proper channels, with the right people being informed at all times especially those in line management. Short circuiting the established communication network will inevitably get the training section condemned as an espionage organization. Once a concern becomes defensive and entrenched in its attitude towards training, particularly if it becomes cynical about training objectives, then the power for change is drastically reduced.

Since in many ways the training section acts as a model to new employees, the ethical standards of behaviour within the department should be maintained at an exemplary level. The norms that are set will obviously originate in high places, but all people who choose, or are chosen, to teach others should bear in mind their parental role in standard setting.

Lastly, trainers have potential to spot the high-flier, that rare genius that all organizations own from time to time. (As Bernard Berenson says: 'We define genius as the capacity for productive reaction against one's training.') The power to spot this ability and to channel special aptitudes at an early stage is one of the most valuable contributions to overall efficiency that the trainer can make.

INDEX

Absenteeism, 3
Abuse of equipment, 10
Accident rates, 3
Action-centred groups, 94
Administration of training, 141
Administration of training, checklist, 170
Age as a factor in learning, 28
Agencies, government training, 155
Aides-memoire, 91
Algorithms, 90
Allocation of training roles, 6
Analysis, job, 36, 165
Analysis, task, 165
Analysis, faults, 117
Anxiety, as a factor in learning, 27
Appearance, of trainer, 97
Appraisal, 80, 122
Assessment, methods of, 60
Assessment of management training needs, 125
Assessment training needs checklist, 163
Assignments, 92

BACIE, 160
Bar charts, 114
Behavioural objectives, 53, 110
Blackboards, 64
Boards, 64
Bottlenecks, in production, 10, 138
Branching programmes, 88
Breakdown, left hand/right hand, 47
Breakdown, task, 46
Business games, 85

Case study, 81

Checklists, 103, 162
'Chinagraph' pencils, 72
Choosing the right method, 167
City and Guilds of London Institute, 117
Closed circuit TV, 71
Coaching, 122
Cognitor processes, 15
Colleges, 124
Columnar training plans, 32
Commencement in lesson planning, 55
Communications, 71, 86
Complaints, 10
Concepts, rate of introduction, 77, 80
Conclusion in lesson planning, 60
Consultant trainers, 124
Core, in lesson planning, 57
Core-competency of trainers, 152
Costs, of training, 133, 134
Counselling, 80
Criterion|behaviour in objectives, 53

D-groups, 94
Daily programme, 117
Decreasing gains in skill pick-up, 19
Demonstration and practice, 83, 84
Depth of impression in learning, 17
Development, management, 121
Diagnosis, faults, 119
Diploma in Management Studies, 124
Discussion, group, 78, 79, 108
Display summaries, 62
Do-it-yourself learning, checklist, 167
Duties, on job description, 41

173

Index

Earnings, estimated, as an incentive, 115
Effector processes, 15
Emphasis, in use of voice, 97
Employment Services Agency, 56
Encouragement, 25
Epidiascope, 68
Ethics, trainer's, 171
Evaluation, of quality of training, 132
Evaluation, of training costs, 133
Exercises, 86
Existence needs in motivation, 24
Experienced Worker Standard (EWS), 20, 112, 133
Experiential learning, 88, 92
Exposure, training by, 2
Extrinsic motivation, 23
Eye contact, 97

Faults analysis, 117
Fault correction, 10
Fault diagnosis, 117
Fear of failure, 27
Feedback, importance of, 24
Film, 66
Filmstrips, 67
First line management, 125
Flannelboard, 65
Flap sequences, 70
Flipchart, 69
Format, in job description, 39
Fulfilment of personal targets, 25
Future training needs, 9

Glossary of Training Terms (HMSO), 122
Goal setting, 23
Grant, ITB, 157
Graphs, quality, 113
Graphs, time/performance, 111
Group discussions, 79
Group dynamics, 93

'Hand-outs', 102
Headings, in job description, 39

Hearing, 12
How trainees learn, checklist, 163

Identification of training needs, 7
Inaccurate records, 10
Incentives in learning, 25
Industrial Society, The, 160
Industrial Training Board (ITB), 6, 40, 117, 124, 130, 157
Institute of Personnel Management (IPM), 149, 161
Institute of Training Officers (ITO), 149, 161
Instructional objectives, 52
Instructional schedules, 54
Instructional technique, 96, 168
Instructor training and selection, 80, 146, 147
Interactive training, 77, 94
Interest, creation of, 55
Interviewing, 80
In-tray exercises, 86
Intrinsic motivation, 23

Job analysis, 7
Jobcentres, 156
Job definition, 38
Job description, 8, 38
Job rotation, 122
Job specification, 41
Judgement, in learning, 15

Key areas, 11
Kinaesthesis, 13
Knowledge analysis, 44
Knowledge, imparting, 74
Knowledge, instruction checklist, 106
Knowledge of results, 16, 110

Laboratory training, 94
Labour turnover, 136
Learning curves, 19
Learning, factors affecting, 16
Learning process, 12
Lecture, 74

Index

Length, of practice sessions, 16
Lesson, 77
Levy, ITB, 157
Linear programmes, 88
Link trainers, 84
Loop projector, 67

Magnetic board, 64
Management by objectives (MBO), 123
Management centres, 123
Management development, 121
Management games, 85
Management training, 81
Manner, in instruction, 96
Mannerisms, distracting, 96
Manpower Services Commission, 155
Manuals, training, 141
Methods, Time, Measurement (MTM), 49
Middle manager's training needs, 126
Mock-ups, 84
Model, the trainer as a, 26
Models, 72
Monitoring performance, 110, 164
Monthly reports, 117
Motivation in learning, 23

National Examinations Board in Supervisory Studies (NEBSS), 124
Negative transfer in learning, 18
Newsprint, 69
Nomograph, 115
Norms, of training section, 172
Note-taking, 60

Objectives, behavioural, 53, 110
Objectives, instructional, 52
Observation in job analysis, 37
Observing groups, 94
Older workers, 28
On-job aids, 72
On-job trainers, 146

Organizational skills, 86
Organizing training, 143
Overlearning, 21
Overhead projects (OHP), 68
Overhead recovery, 136

Pace of instruction, 97
Part versus whole learning, 16
Participation, in learning, 59
Pause in instruction, 97
Pegboard, 65
Perception in learning, 13
Perception, factors affecting levels of, 14
Performance monitoring, 110
Planning training, 30
Planning, checklist, 165
Planned development, 122
Plastigraph boards, 65
Plateaux on learning curves, 20
Policy, formulation of training, 6
Policy, management development, 121
Preparation of instructional material, 52, 166
Process in groups, 93
Professional associations, 161
Programmed instruction, 88
Programmes, design of, 32, 34
Programmes, training, 31
Programmes, writing for 'teaching machines', 89
Progress charts, 116
Project, 92
Projected aids, 65
Psychomotor skills, 87
Punishment, 26

Qualities of a successful trainer, 26
Quality graphs, 113
Quality rating, 112
Questioning, technique during teaching, 98
Questionnaires, 162
Questions in assessing training needs, 8

175

Index

Rating, performance, 112
Recapitulation, 162
Receptor processes, 12
Records of courses attended, 131
Records, design and location of, 132
Records, financial, 131
Records, training, 131
Recruitment, 137
Reduction of learning time, 3, 134
Reject rates, 10
'Relatedness' needs in motivation, 24
Relationship, trainer/trainee, 26
Remedial training, 10
Reviewing training, 139
Role play, 71, 80

Safety, 10
Sales training, 80, 91, 146
Scrap rates, 135
Seminars, 75
Sensitivity training, 94
Sensorimotor skills, 15
Sequence in instruction, 103
Sequence in learning, 17, 58
Session plans, 54
Sight, 12
Simulation, 84
Skillcentres, 158
'Skills analysis', 48
Skills, analysis of, 45
Skills, instruction of, 83
Skills, instruction, checklist, 104
Skills, social, 8, 43, 71, 78
Slide projector, 66
Smell, 13
Social skills, 8, 43, 71, 78
Stage I analysis, 45
Stage II analysis, 47
Stage III analysis, 47
Stamina build up, 34
Strategy, choice of, 74
Supervisory training, 81, 125, 129
Syllabus, management training, 127
Systematic training, benefits of, 3

T-groups, 94

Talks, 77
Target setting, 111
Task analysis, 44
Task analysis, benefit of, 49
Teaching machines, 88
Teaching questions, 98
Terminal behaviour in objectives, 53
Testing questions, 98
Timed targets, 111
Time graphs, 111
Touch, 12
Trainee's notes, 101
Training, aims and definition of, 2
Training, administration of, 141, 144
Training department, duties of, 144
Training forecast, 10
Training manuals, 141
Training needs, 9, 10, 126
Training officer, duties of, 143
Training officer, selection and training, 148
Training of Trainers Committee (TSD), 151
Training Opportunity Scheme (TOPS), 156, 158
Training organization, 143
Training organizations (voluntary), 160, 171
Training policy checklist, 162
Training programmes, 31
Training records, 130
Training review, 138
Training supervisors checklist, 169
Training Services Agency/Division, 150, 155
Training Within Industry (TWI), 46, 103, 147, 159
Transparencies, OHP, 69
Tutorials, 76

Video-tape recorders (VTR), 71
Visual aids, 63
Voice, use of in instruction, 97
Volume in use of voice, 97
Voluntary Training Organizations, 160

Index

Wall charts, 70
Wastage, 3, 10
Weekly reports, 117
Whiteboards, 64

Why trainees learn, checklist, 164
Working models, 69
Working needs and satisfactions, 24
Worksheet, fault analysis, 118